Contents

Foreword

This book is based on the Yachtmaster* Ocean syllabus of the governing body of sailing in the United Kingdom, the Royal Yachting Association. It assumes that the reader is a competent sailor and coastal navigator with a basic knowledge of meteorology and chartwork.

There is no end to the text that could be written about ocean sailing, from poetry books to works on electronics and boat-fixing. This volume concentrates on the absolute essentials that separate ocean sailing from all other facets of small craft seafaring. None of the subjects requires a higher degree of learning than the average teenager has acquired by the age of fourteen.

Success on the wide ocean depends on straight thinking and self-reliance but, like all forms of education, these are best built on solid principles. The RYA* has created a realistic syllabus for today's sailors. This book brings it to the reader in a form that should be as much use at sea in foul weather as it is in a warm classroom safe at home. Enjoy it, persevere with the new concepts, and a cracking fair wind to you when next you set sail.

Part I: Celestial Navigation

Introduction

*NAVIGATION is that art which instructs
the mariner in what manner to conduct
a ship through the wide and trackless ocean,
from one part to another,
with the greatest safety, and in the
shortest time possible.*

*J W Norie
Norie's Practical Navigation
(mid-nineteenth century)*

Ocean navigation has changed utterly in the twenty-five years between my first venture across the Atlantic as skipper and my most recent crossing of the same stretch of water. From celestial navigation as the only option, we have stumbled through a dawn period of transit satellites into the full daylight of universal GPS. If the bulkhead GPS fails for any reason out on the wide ocean, the skipper simply reaches into his kitbag for the backup unit he bought at the boat show for the price of his night's lodging. Those whose experience of technology has presented a catalogue of disappointment may even have invested in more than two such wonders.

Since the beginnings of seafaring, mankind has navigated under the inescapable reality that for much of the time his position was seen through a frosted window. All at once, technology has leapt ahead, and an exact fix is available whenever we desire it. For the foreseeable future, therefore, mainstream navigators will use GPS as their primary fixing tool. Celestial navigation is deposed from its hitherto unassailable situation at the summit of the navigator's achievement. Overnight, the

skills of the ages have been degraded to mere back-up against the ultimate catastrophe, loss of volts. For many sailors, however, the change is to be lamented as well as welcomed.

Until a few years ago, you would have plunged into the Celestial Navigation section of the Yachtmaster Ocean syllabus in earnest, for without it, you would have been truly lost while off soundings. Except in emergency, this is no longer the case, but it does not mean that when things are going smoothly on the electronic front the old ways should be consigned to an unvisited corner of the mind.

First, there is a spiritual aspect to the regular use of the sextant. Only the most cynical never felt a tingle of pure awe at the thought that they had fixed their position to within a mile or two on the planet we call home by observations of stars and galaxies marching in silence through the infinity of space. This daily connection with the heavens used to serve as a constant reminder of our own ultimate insignificance - no bad thing for a seaman, or anyone else for that matter. Together with this metaphysical aspect to astro-navigation came a constant uncertainty about one's position which bred seamanlike caution. When finally dispelled by a good landfall, this gave rise to an elation that no longer has a parallel. All this is potentially lost to the electronic navigator.

Of greater concern to some, however, will be that sextant work, like all arts, requires continuous practice to achieve any real proficiency. Buying the book and the instrument isn't enough. Nor is it sufficient to take a couple of sun sights on a long passage and send them to an examiner who may then declare you an Ocean Yachtmaster. The traditional daily round of morning or evening stars and the forenoon sight of the sun followed by a noon latitude not only gave rhythm to the watch system, it also bred a facility with the tools that today's

navigator will still need if the magic box ever goes down.

For all these reasons, any skipper of a yacht on the ocean should make the effort to master celestial navigation. The methods and techniques have been set out here in a form that will get you navigating by the sky as soon as possible - long before you have finished the book - but do not for one moment suppose that because the Sun makes its appearance in these pages before the stars that it is more important. You have to start somewhere and the Sun is pretty hard to miss, so it's the best thing on which to practise using your sextant. It won't help you much though, if you are expecting a dawn landfall on an unlit coast and you are wondering where you are, because it won't be around to be observed until after breakfast. Instead, morning stars and a planet or two thrown in for good measure will, if the sky is clear, fix your position to within a mile or so. As you will see, stars are surprisingly easy to operate with, the planets are a delight to identify and simple to reduce, and even the Moon, smiling wryly down on our efforts, can provide a useful signpost.

I am not an astronomer. I am by no stretch of the imagination either a physicist or a mathematician. I am, before everything, a practical seaman. I have learned navigation the easy way, by spending long periods of time at sea. One by one I have forced myself over the hurdles presented in my mind by planets, Moon and stars and found on each occasion that what I imagined to be a problem soluble only by the academic or hard-line professional turned out to be yet another piece of cake.

The whole business, if tackled in the right order, is amazingly simple. In the following chapters I have set out from my own experience what you need to know. Very little more, and no less. You'll notice that Chapter 1 is all about concepts, conventions and definitions. `In the beginning was The Word'. Skip it, and you're in trouble. Read it, understand it and be ready to refer back to it because it is the rock on which the rest is built. Once you're over Chapter 1, which should be interesting if only for the new perspective on your surroundings, the rest of the book will be pure joy. So welcome to the World of the Enlightened. Fair winds to you on your voyage!

1 The Earth and the heavens

At school we all learn that the Earth revolves once a day and that the stars remain, to a greater or lesser extent, stationary. We also learn that the Moon is in our own back yard, that the stars are plunging through space at various mind-boggling distances from us and that the Earth is travelling on an annual voyage around the Sun. Whether or not all this is true is of no relevance to the practical astro-navigator. For our purposes the Earth, otherwise known as the *terrestrial sphere*, is a perfectly round ball swimming in a vacuum at the centre of the known universe.

At the outside of the vacuum, an indeterminate but fortunately irrelevant distance away, is the big ball which marks the perimeter of the universe. This ball is known as the *celestial sphere*. For our purposes all the heavenly bodies move in their courses on its inside surface, and its centre coincides exactly with the centre of the Earth.

Any location on the Earth's surface can be expressed in terms of latitude and longitude.

Meridians of longitude

To define our position on the globe in an east-west direction we make use of the meridians of longitude. These, you will recall, are great circles which converge at the poles of the Earth, a great circle being the line described on the Earth's surface by a plane passing through the centre of the Earth. Any great circle must have equal halves in the northern and southern hemispheres, and its points of greatest latitude are called its *Vertices* (singular, *Vertex*). At the vertex, it is making a tangent to the adjacent parallel of latitude and is thus travelling briefly east-west.

We measure our position in terms of *angular distance* east or west of the zero° or datum meridian. This passes through the Greenwich Observatory in England, and is therefore known as the *Greenwich Meridian*.

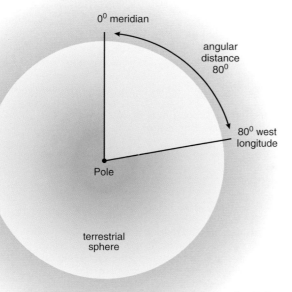

Looking down on the Earth's axis from the Pole. *An observer at 80°W longitude is at an angular distance of 80° west of the Greenwich Meridian.*

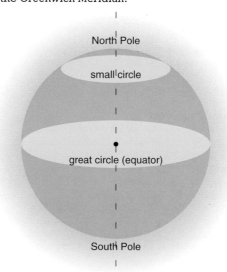

Great and small circles (Earth viewed from just north of the equator). *The equator is a great circle - that is, on a plane that passes through the centre of the Earth - but all the other parallels of latitude are small circles.*

Parallels of latitude

Having determined our angular distance east or west of Greenwich we need another set of co-ordinates to fix us in a north/south direction. These are the parallels of latitude, which define our angular distance north or south of the *equator*, which is the great circle on a plane at right angles to the Earth's axis, halfway between two poles.

The equator is the only parallel of latitude which fulfils the definition of a great circle. All the others are *small circles* (see diagram).

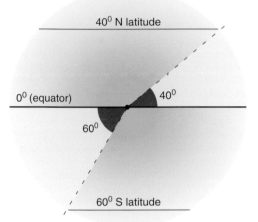

Latitude - the Earth (the terrestrial sphere) viewed from the plane of the equator. *Latitude is expressed as an angular distance north or south of the equator, measured from the centre of the Earth.*

Geographic position

Any point on the Earth's surface fixed by its *terrestrial co-ordinates* (latitude and longitude), is known as a *geographic position* (GP).

Angular distance

Distances between locations on Earth are generally expressed in miles or kilometres. This is convenient because we need to time our journeys. But for the purposes of celestial navigation the most convenient unit of distance is a degree of the 360° circle. It would be impossible to try to handle the north/south distance between Sirius and Aldebaran in terms of miles, but to say that it is 33° measured from the centre of the Earth is quite comprehensible and very easy to work with.

Subdivision of degrees

A degree subdivides into 60 minutes (60'), and each minute into 60 seconds (60"). By a wonderful coincidence (or is it?) one minute of

The celestial sphere is an imaginary sphere enclosing the Earth, with its own poles and equator. *For the purposes of navigation, all celestial bodies such as the Sun and the stars are positioned on the surface of this sphere regardless of their actual distance from the Earth.*

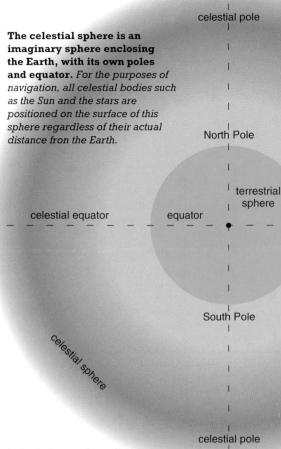

latitude is equal, at all latitudes, to one nautical mile (1M). One second of latitude is equal to 101 feet, or three boat lengths for the average yacht. Since this is clearly too small to be of any serious use, minutes of arc are subdivided into decimal points, thus: 36° 14.1' N.

One minute of longitude equals one mile at the equator, but diminishes to zero at the poles. Working out what it represents in between in terms of miles would mean yet another sum, so there, straight away, is a very good reason for the concept of angular distance.

The Celestial Sphere

Just as it is possible to fix a position on the Earth's surface using its terrestrial co-ordinates of latitude and longitude, so the exact situation of a heavenly body on the surface of the celestial sphere can be defined by its *celestial co-ordinates*.

All the main features of the terrestrial sphere are mirrored in its celestial counterpart.

The terrestrial poles, if projected outwards from the centre of the Earth onto the celestial sphere, form the *celestial poles*. The terrestrial equator is projected outwards to throw a 'great circle' onto the celestial sphere equidistant at all points from the celestial poles. This is called the *celestial equator*.

Celestial longitude
- or Greenwich Hour Angle (GHA)

Since the first edition of this book, the notion of Greenwich Mean Time (GMT) has been replaced by Universal Time (UT). You may well find that modern almanacs and data in general refer to UT. The tables here refer to GMT for publishing convenience. There is no practical difference between the two.

The *celestial zero meridian* is the projection of the terrestrial zero (Greenwich) meridian. However, whereas terrestrial longitude is measured from the Greenwich meridian in degrees *east* or *west* around the world to 180° on the opposite side, celestial longitude, which

is known as Greenwich Hour Angle (GHA), is measured to the westward **only** in degrees from 0° to 360°. When considering matters concerning the concept of Greenwich Hour Angle, never forget that it is merely a way of expressing celestial longitude.

You will see in the diagram below that 40°W longitude is the equivalent of a GHA of 40° on the celestial sphere, and that 120° E longitude marries up with GHA 240°. A second glance will show that if 120°E were expressed in a 0° to 360° notation, beginning at Greenwich and working westward, it would represent a longitude of 240°. It is just a question of convention and, for better or worse, longitude is expressed as 0° to 180° east or west, and GHA as 0° to 360°.

To convert east longitude to 360° notation and tie it in with the corresponding GHA, simply subtract the figure from 360°. Thus 120° east is equivalent to a GHA of 360 minus 120, or 240°.

To find the GHA of a body for a given time (and it changes by the second as the Earth turns) you need to consult the daily pages of *The Nautical Almanac*. Illustrated on pages 30-31 is the pair of daily pages for 1st, 2nd and 3rd of May 1986. You will see that on the right-hand page the far left column refers to hours of GMT and the next column gives the GHA of the Sun for the hour *exactly*. To find the increment by which it varies for minutes and seconds of time, you turn to the 'increments' tables in the back pages of the almanac, an example of which is illustrated on page 32, and read off the answer, making sure that you take it from the correct column.

Note that since the heavenly bodies are moving westward, their GHA goes on increasing until it reads 360°, when it starts again. This means that you always *add* the minutes and seconds increment to the hourly value of the GHA.

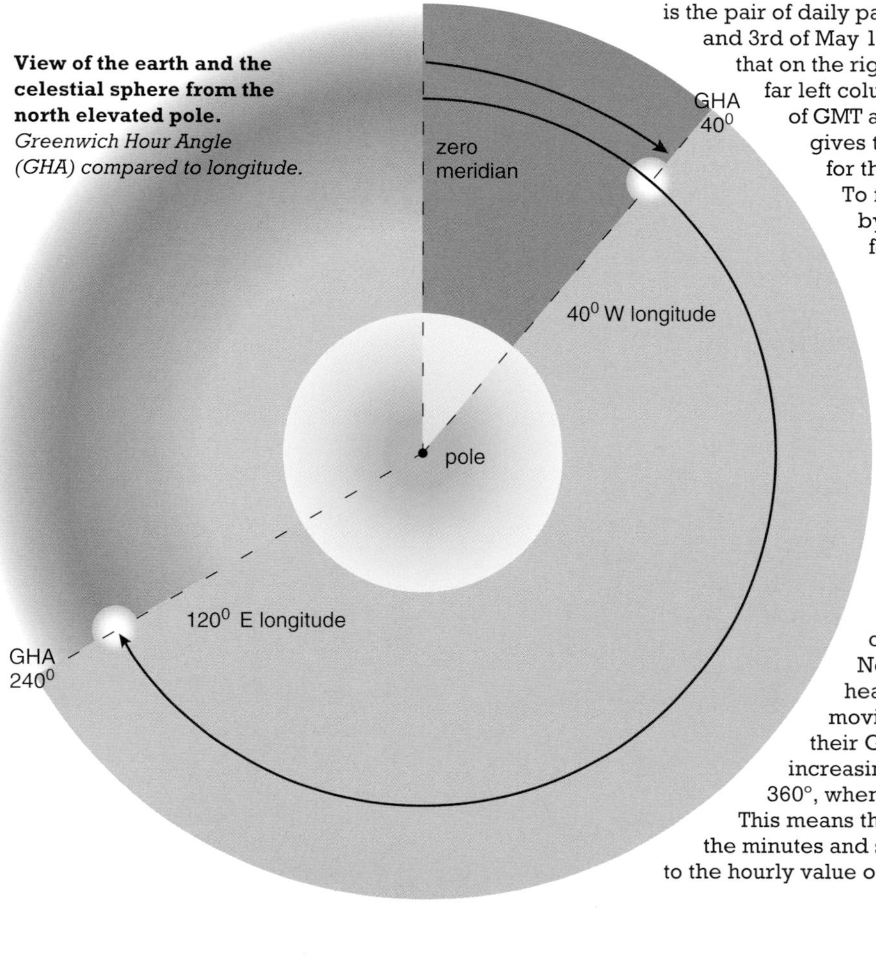

View of the earth and the celestial sphere from the north elevated pole.
Greenwich Hour Angle (GHA) compared to longitude.

GHA 40°

zero meridian

40° W longitude

pole

120° E longitude

GHA 240°

Example

What is the GHA of the Sun at 10h 15m 47s GMT on May 1st 1986?

GHA 10h	330° 43′	.5
+ Increment for 15m 47s	3° 56′	.8
GHA Sun	334° 40′	.3

Notice that 43'.5 + 56'.8 equals 1° 40'.3. You only have to get to 60 minutes to make one degree.

Celestial latitude, or declination

The cross co-ordinate used on the celestial sphere to fix the position of a heavenly body north or south on its GHA co-ordinate is its *declination*. As you will by now be able to predict, it corresponds exactly to terrestrial latitude.

Declination is actually angular distance north or south of the celestial equator and, like terrestrial latitude, it is conveniently named north or south.

A body with a *declination* of 42°N will, at some time in the 24-hour period, pass directly over the head of an observer in 42°N latitude.

To calculate the declination of a body for a given time you need once more to consult the almanac.

Look again at the daily pages illustration (pages 30-31) and notice that each column gives not only the changing GHA of the body, but also its declination.

At the bottom of the column is a small letter 'd' with a numerical value beside it. This is the rate of change per hour. Inspection of the hours adjacent to the one you are interested in will show whether the change is to be added or subtracted, depending on whether declination is increasing or decreasing.

If you look now at the illustration of the 'increments' page (page 32), you will see a column for each minute headed 'v' or 'd' correction.

Suppose you are interested in a 14-minute increment and a 'd' value of + 0.9. You go down the column for 14 minutes until you come to 'd' 0.9 and read off the value, which is + 0.2. It is this figure that you add to the hourly declination figure you have taken from the daily page. Notice that 'v' and 'd' corrections do not refer to seconds of time. The figures in the column are for minutes only, which is invariably quite accurate enough.

In practice, you can usually work out the declination for a given number of minutes after the hour by inspection and mental arithmetic, so recourse to the increment pages for changing declination is rare.

Earth and the celestial sphere from the equator. Latitude compared to declination.

In the case of the Moon, however, declination varies rapidly and hugely and the mental arithmetic involved in bypassing the 'd' increment is way beyond me. Here, then, is an example of its use:

Example

What is the declination of the Moon at 2314 on 3rd May 1986?

Dec 23h	S 8° 15′ .3
-d(14.4) 14m	3′ .5
Dec 2314	S 8° 11′ .8

Note that in this case 'd' is negative because declination is decreasing, and that the declination is always labelled N or S.

Zenith

An observer's *zenith* is his terrestrial position projected (from the centre of the Earth) onto the celestial sphere. In other words, the point directly above his head. The declination of his zenith is the same as his latitude. The GHA of his zenith is the same as his longitude. (Although in east longitude it will be necessary to adjust the longitude figure to read 0° to 360° notation by subtracting it from 360°.)

Opposite the observer's zenith is the celestial position delightfully termed his *nadir*. Project a line from his zenith through the observer to the centre of the Earth, keep going until you hit the celestial sphere on the other side, and you have it. As the name suggests, it's about as low as you can get.

Local Hour Angle

In the majority of the calculations involved in celestial nagivation you will need to use not the Greenwich Hour Angle of the body concerned, but the *Local Hour Angle* (LHA).

Just as the GHA of the body at a given time

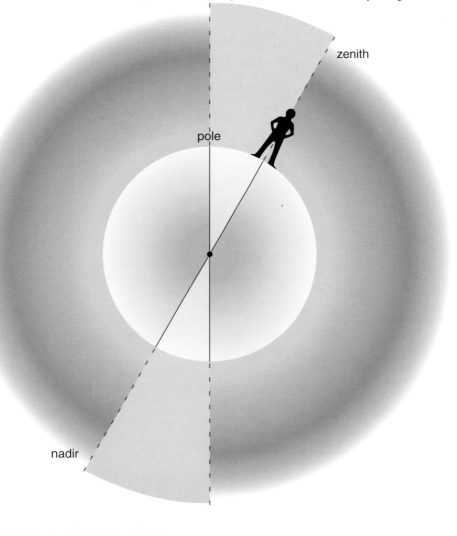

zenith

pole

nadir

is its angular distance west of the *Greenwich* meridian, so the LHA of the same body is its angular distance to the west of the *observer's* meridian.

Given that you have extracted the GHA of the body from the almanac (see page 9) and you have some idea of your longitude, you should have no difficulty in working out the body's approximate LHA.

As always with angular questions, when in doubt draw a diagram. Below are four examples with diagrams to illustrate the four most likely calculations of LHA. They are quite simple and it is vital that they are understood. Without a grasp of the concept of Local Hour Angle, the rest of the book may as well be written in Hottentot for all the good it will do you.

Case 1

West longitude: GHA of Sun greater than observer's longitude.
In this case
LHA = GHA minus longitude west.

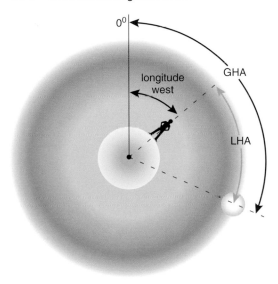

Example What is the LHA of the Sun at 16h 15m 27s GMT on 1st May 1986? Your longitude is 15° 23′W.

GHA 16h	60°	43′	.9
+ Increment 15m 27s	3°	51′	.8
GHA Sun	64°	35′	.7
—Longitude west	15°	23′	.0
LHA	49°	12′	.7

Case 2

West Longitude: GHA less than observer's longitude
If you study the diagram, you'll see that the logical answer in this case is to find the difference between the longitude west and the GHA and then subtract it from 360 (the remainder of the full circle).

On the face of it, this looks a bit awkward. By far the easiest way to handle it is to add the GHA to 360 and then subtract the west longitude. The answer comes out right every time.

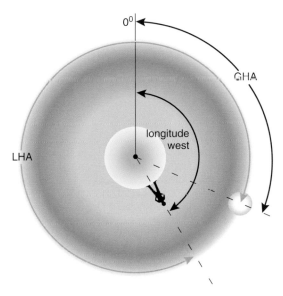

Example What is the LHA of the Sun at 14h 16m 18s GMT on Tuesday 3rd May 1986? Your longitude is 40° 13′W.

GHA 14h	30°	47′	.2
+ Increment 16m 18s	4°	04′	.5
GHA Sun	34°	51′	.7
+ 360	360°		
GHA + 360	394°	51′	.7
-Longitude west	40°	13′	.0
LHA	354°	38′	.7

In both examples, LHA = GHA minus longitude west. If longitude west happens to be greater than LHA and makes the sum a nonsense, just remember to add a quick 360° where it counts and all will be well.

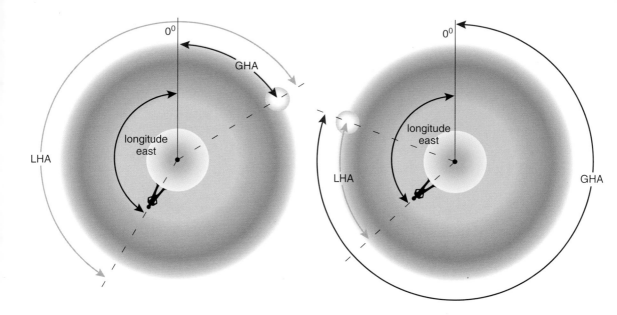

Case 3

East longitude: GHA a smaller value than the longitude (expressed in 360° notation).
A glance at the diagram makes this one obvious, remembering always that LHA is the angular distance of the body from the observer, moving to the westward (clockwise on the diagram). In this case LHA = GHA + longitude east.

Example What is the LHA of the Sun at 03h 15m 22s on May 1st 1986? Your longitude is 110°E.

GHA 03h	225°	42′	.9
+ Increment 15m 22s	3°	50′	.5
GHA Sun	229°	33′	.4
+ Longitude east	110°		
LHA Sun	339°	33′	.4

Case 4

East longitude: GHA a greater value than longitude (expressed in 360° notation).

This case is easier than a first glance at the diagram might suggest. You are looking for the angular distance to the westward between the observer and the Sun or star. One way to do this is to work your longitude into 360° notation and subtract it from the GHA, but the easiest way is to add up the GHA and the longitude expressed conventionally as degrees east (of Greenwich). The sum of the two will be greater than 360° which is a nonsense, but if you subtract 360° from the result, you will have the right answer.

Example What is the LHA of the Sun at 02h 17m 28s on May 3rd 1986? Your longitude is 172° 15′E.

GHA 02h	210°	46′	.4
+ Increment 17m 28s	4°	22′	.0
GHA Sun	215°	08′	.4
+ Longitude east	172°	15′	.0
	387°	23′	.4
—360	360°		
LHA Sun	27°	23′	.4

General rules

From the above examples you'll see that two general rules are applicable when working out LHA.

If you are in west longitude **LHA = GHA minus longitude west**. If GHA is a smaller figure than longitude west, just add 360° to it and carry on. It's as simple as that.
If you are in east longitude **LHA = GHA plus longitude east**. If the answer turns out to be greater than 360°, subtract 360° from it and there is the LHA.

Got it? Good, then carry on.

HORIZON

One final concept. Every schoolchild knows what the horizon is. Or thinks he does. There's just a bit more to it than that for the navigator. All astro-navigation depends upon observing

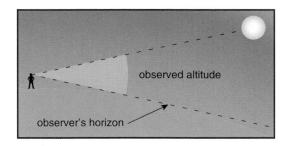

the 'altitudes' of the Sun, Moon, stars and planets. The altitudes are measured with a sextant and can only be observed as the angle at the observer between the heavenly body and the observer's horizon.

All the navigational tables work on the assumption that the observer with his sextant is at the centre of the terrestrial sphere, and not on the Earth's surface.

Because the Earth has a measurable size, at least in comparison with the distance to the Moon, the Sun and some of the planets, this discrepancy leads to an error of parallax between what he is actually seeing (the terrestrial or 'corrected' visual horizon) and what the tables want him to see (the celestial horizon).

This error is called *horizontal parallax*. It can be as much as one degree in the case of the Moon, which in consequence requires its own correction table, but it reduces to a fraction of

a minute for the Sun and the planets and, as you will see, is very easily dealt with.

The size of the Earth when related to the distance to the nearest star is a pitiful irrelevance so, when working up starsights, parallax is non-existent.

For purposes of calculation, what we are after is the angle (measured at the centre of the Earth) between the celestial horizon and the altitude of the Sun, Moon, star or planet.

The *celestial horizon* is on a plane constructed at right angles to a vertical line dropped from the position of the observer to the centre of the Earth.

The observer cannot see this horizon. What he can see (with a few small adjustments) is the *terrestrial horizon*. This is a plane drawn as a tangent to the Earth's surface and is at right angles to the line joining the observer, his zenith and the centre of the Earth.

Because the observer's eye will be above the surface of the Earth by anything from six feet in a small yacht to a hundred in a large tanker he is obviously going to see 'over the edge' and beyond the terrestrial horizon to his *visual horizon*. The angular inaccuracy thus caused is called *dip* and is taken care of by a small angular corrective factor given in the almanac.

Don't get concerned about horizons and parallax. In practice they present no difficulties at all.

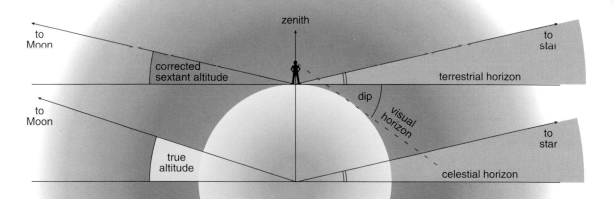

Owing to the close proximity of the Moon, there is a difference between its corrected sextant altitude and its true altitude from the centre of the Earth. Stars, on the other hand, are so far away that the sextant altitude and true altitude are effectively the same.

2   The sextant

In the last chapter I let slip that all astro-navigation depends upon observing the angle between the horizon and the heavenly body of your choice. Methods of achieving this measurement have improved no end over the years. The tenth-century Vikings, including Bjarni Herjolfsson, the discoverer of America, used to measure the altitude of Polaris using a notched stick. This gave them a crude comparative latitude without involving them in discussions about whether or not the world was round.

Today we have the sextant. It is so called because its calibrated arc is one-sixth of a circle, or 60°. By the doubling effect of its mirrors it is actually able to measure angles of up to 120°. This represents a big leap forward from its predecessor the octant, which has an arc of one-eighth of a circle, doubles up to only 90° and has thus been retired from active service to languish in picturesque obscurity on pub walls.

HOW THE SEXTANT WORKS

If you look at the sextant illustrated, or better still hold yours in your hand, you will see that

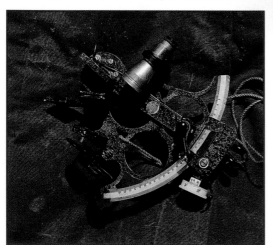

The tool of the trade: the sextant. You don't have to buy one like this - you can get cheap plastic ones that work very well, although they may need adjusting more often.

it consists of a frame with a handle, a moving 'index arm' with a mirror at one end and a micrometer at the other, and a fixed mirror upon which the telescope appears to focus.

Look more closely at the fixed mirror and you will see that it consists of two halves. One half is mirror, and the other is clear glass. That is the

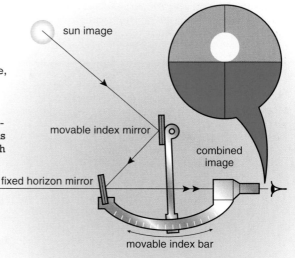

The index bar of the sextant is slid along the arc until the index mirror reflects the Sun's image onto the horizon mirror. When the two images coincide as shown, the reading on the arc represents the sextant altitude of the Sun.

secret of the instrument. Light from the heavenly body is reflected by the index mirror down onto the horizon mirror, which reflects it through the telescope to your eye. If the instrument is set up so that you are seeing the horizon through the plain glass with the reflected image of the heavenly body apparently 'sitting' on it, the sextant will tell you the angle between them.

SETTING UP THE SEXTANT

The first thing to do when you buy a sextant is to splice a lanyard to it to go around your neck. The next thing is to remove the telescope, focus it on infinity (the horizon) to suit your good eye, and then replace it.

Once you can see through the device properly you can *adjust* it to remove the various errors. These are as follows:

Perpendicularity

Effect: Images side by side.

Cause: Index and horizon mirrors out of parallel.

Cure: You need to adjust the index mirror. Look across the sextant so that you can see the image of the arc in the index mirror adjacent to the actual arc, as shown in the illustration. To arrange this you'll have to set the index bar to something like 60°. If the real arc will not run perfectly into its image without a 'step', this shows that there is an error of perpendicularity. You can remove it by adjusting the screw in the back of the index mirror with the tool provided. The index mirror is now 'true'.

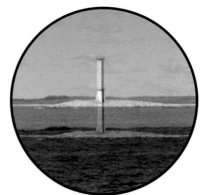

Side error.
If you can place the images one on top of the other like this then there is no side error in the sextant.

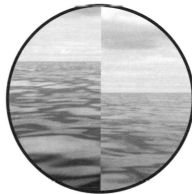

Index error.
The sextant is set at zero, but despite this there is a step in the horizon line, indicating an index error. To deal with this, adjust the vertical alignment screw on the horizon mirror, checking the effect by sighting on the horizon line (below).

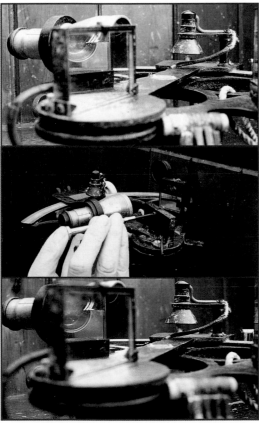

Perpendicularity. *This sextant has an error of perpendicularity, shown by the reflection of the arc in the index mirror (centre of top picture). The cure for this is to adjust the mirror (centre picture) until the arc and its reflection run into each other without a step (lower picture).*

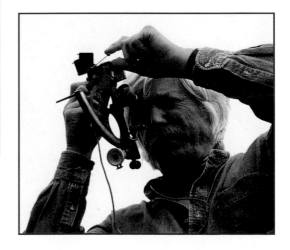

Side error (see left)

Effect: Images side by side.
Cause: Since the index mirror is now 'proved', the error must lie in the horizon mirror.
Cure: First set the instrument to zero. The horizon mirror has two adjusting screws. To take out side error you should set up the screw which moves the mirror across, rather than up and down. It will be found at one side of the mirror. Don't worry if this produces a large 'index error' (up and down error) because the last adjustment for index error should remove this.

Index error (see left)

Effect: Images one above the other with the instrument set at zero.
Cause: Horizon mirror out of adjustment in the 'up and down' plane.
Cure: Adjust the second screw on the horizon mirror. You may find that this will reintroduce a little side error; a small error can be tolerated, but by playing one adjustment against the other you may still be able to eliminate both.

If you cannot, then you are stuck with an *index error*. This, in practice, will not vary with a good instrument and once quantified should be allowed for each time you use the sextant.

To quantify your index error, look at a star or the horizon through the instrument and place the two images exactly side by side. Then read the sextant. The reading on the micrometer is the index error. It should not be more than two or three minutes and should be labelled *on* or *off* the arc.

If the sextant is reading + 2 minutes (say), then your index error is on the arc and should be subtracted from all your subsequent readings to render them true. If the instrument is reading 58 minutes, then your error is two minutes *off* the arc and you should add two minutes to your readings. To sum up:

When it's **OFF** (the arc), add it **ON**.
When it's **ON** take it **OFF**.

TRUE ALTITUDE AND SEXTANT ALTITUDE

Having set up your sextant you know that it is giving the correct altitude for the body - given the possible regular correction for index error. Unless you bounce it, it should remain true for years without further attention. Just check it over once in a while.

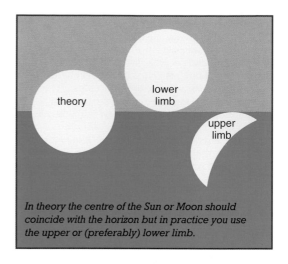

In theory the centre of the Sun or Moon should coincide with the horizon but in practice you use the upper or (preferably) lower limb.

In order to reduce the altitude you measure with your sextant to the true altitude of the body (that is the angle it is making with the *celestial* horizon) you need to make a few corrections - on paper this time.

Dip

Just to recap, this is the correction to be applied because your height of eye enables you to see beyond the theoretical terrestrial horizon.

In the front of *The Nautical Almanac*, and on the handout bookmark in every copy, is a group of tables for correcting your sextant altitude. You will see the corrections for dip at the right-hand side of the table on page 35. If you estimate your height of eye to be, for example, 10 feet or three metres, then the correction for dip will be minus 3.1 minutes.
Note: *Dip is always subtractive.*

Waves and dip

It is normal on the ocean to have a sea running. In the northeast trades in mid-Atlantic there will probably be a ground swell eight to ten feet in height. In the North Atlantic after heavy weather there could easily be a swell running to 20 feet or more. If this is the case you'll have to estimate the wave height, divide it by two and add the result to your height of eye; you'll only see the horizon from the top of a wave, so that is where you'll be when you take your sight.

Refraction

Because the light from a heavenly body is bent by the Earth's atmosphere, a correction is necessary for refraction. Fortunately this is included, along with parallax and semidiameter (see next page) where there is any, in the altitude correction tables.

Semidiameter

If you are observing the Sun or the Moon, you cannot guess accurately where the centre of the body is, and so you place the upper or lower limb (see illustration page 17) on the horizon. The altitude correction tables include the corrections required to convert one limb or the other to the real altitude of the Sun and, as you will see, the Moon makes its own arrangements. When entering the tables for the Sun, notice the two columns: one for northern summer and one for winter. The lower limb is given in bold type because, for some reason, it is much easier to shoot than the upper limb and so is preferred by everyone.

Parallax

The Moon is a law to itself here and will be discussed in due course. The Sun's parallax is covered by the altitude correction tables and needs to be considered no further.

Don't forget, though, that the two closest planets, Venus and Mars, sometimes produce a touch of parallax themselves. The central table shown on page 35 is the total correction (excluding dip and index error, of course) for the stars and planets, but in its right-hand column is a small additional correction to be made in certain months for the parallax of our nearest neighbours.

Notice that the point of entry into the altitude correction tables is *apparent altitude*. This is your sextant altitude corrected for index error (if any) and dip.

Low altitude sights

When heavenly bodies are observed at altitudes below 10°, the refraction produced by the Earth's atmosphere begins to increase rapidly. In practice, this can produce some unreliable results and you should generally avoid taking such a sight.

Occasionally, however, you'll have no option as it may be all that is on offer. If this is the case, you'll find a special set of correction tables to deal with low altitudes near the front of *The Nautical Almanac*. A further table follows to deal with the effects of unusual atmospheric pressure and temperature. These are negligible in practice at normal altitudes, but if you are shooting something very low down, they begin to bite, so take care.

It all adds up to an unpromising picture. Try to keep your altitudes up above the 10° mark and these difficulties will never arise. Here is an example of a sextant altitude correction for a typical Sun sight (lower limb).

Sextant altitude (Hs)	56° 17′ .5
Index error (IE)	— 2′ .1
Dip (height of eye 12′)	— 3′ .4
Apparent altitude (App alt)	56° 12′ .0
Altitude correction (April-Sept)	+ 15′ .3
True altitude (Ho)	56° 27′ .3

Now an example on the same sextant for a star:

Hs	24° 15′ .8
IE	— 2′ .1
Dip (HE 8′)	— 2′ .7
App alt	24° 11′ .0
Correction	— 2′ .1
Ho	24° 8′ .9

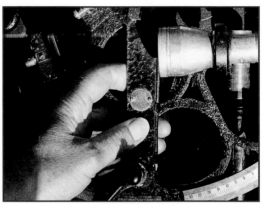

When you pick up the sextant, grasp it by the frame, and not by the index bar, scale or telescope.

USING A SEXTANT

Assuming that your sextant is adjusted correctly, and any index error quantified, this is how you use it to measure the altitude of the Sun.

1 Open the box (right way up).
2 Grasp the instrument, by the frame as far as possible, in your left hand and lift it out of the box. Do *not* lift it by the index bar or by the scale.
3 Take the handle in your right hand and sit yourself comfortably and firmly in a suitable position to take your sight. On a large, stable boat like my pilot cutter you can stand on the deck in clement weather, but sitting is usually preferable. You'll need both hands for the sextant - neither is available for either the ship or yourself, so choose a secure site for your posterior.
4 Set the instrument to 'zero' and look towards the horizon to check the *index error*

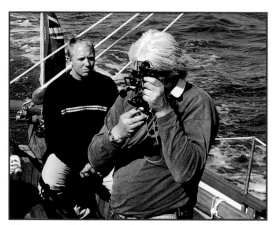

Plant yourself firmly to take a sight.

(see page 17).

5 With the instrument still at zero, drop a shade or two over the index mirror and aim the telescope at the Sun. It may be advisable to put the lightest shade over the horizon mirror as well before you do this, otherwise you could end up with a sore eye.

6 When you have the sun clearly in focus, open the clamp on the index bar with your left hand and, as you sweep the instrument down towards the horizon with your right hand, 'follow' the image of the Sun with your left until it is sitting somewhere near the horizon. This is tricky at first, but it comes with practice.
On all but the brightest days you'll need to remove the shade from the horizon mirror before you use the micrometer to work the Sun's image firmly onto the line of the horizon.

7 It's important that the sextant is exactly

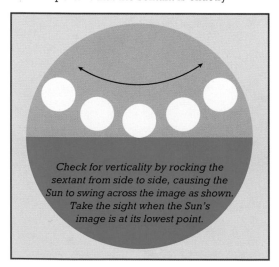

Check for verticality by rocking the sextant from side to side, causing the Sun to swing across the image as shown. Take the sight when the Sun's image is at its lowest point.

vertical when measuring an altitude, so once the sun is approximately in place, you should twist your right wrist from side to side to rock the sextant; as you do this the image of the Sun will appear to 'pendulum' across the horizon. When it is at its lowest point, the sextant is vertical: this is the moment to set the micrometer and read off the altitude.

8 If you catch the Sun at ten o'clock on a midsummer morning its rate of climb will surprise you, but around noon it won't be moving very fast at all, so be ready for both states.

Care of the sextant

Handled carefully, a good sextant requires only minimal day-to-day maintenance. Its moving parts are surprisingly robust, and an occasional drop of light machine oil are all they need. The mirrors are vulnerable to seawater so a rinse-off in fresh water is important if the instrument stops a wave. Try to resist the temptation to polish your sextant at regular intervals, especially if it is a fine brass one. The trouble is that although this makes it look great, it also slowly and steadily wears away the gradations on the scale. By all means shine up the brass telescope if you have one.

Starting out

Use of the sextant is the essence of celestial navigation. If you are ever to be more than marginally competent you will need to be a dab hand with the tools. Sling the sextant in the car, go down to the nearest south-facing beach, and practise, practise, practise. Ignore the wise-guy taunts of the bathers, because you will have the last laugh.

By the time the Sun has set you'll be quite proficient, so treat yourself to a beer and wait for twilight, then see if you can 'pull down' a few stars before night swallows the horizon. Don't worry about which ones they are, just work at the technique.

Only you can teach yourself how to do this, but pretty soon you'll find that you no longer have to start with the sextant at zero. You'll be able to make a guess and look through it in the general direction of the body, then when you have found what you are searching for you can adjust its image down (or up) to the horizon.

The really good news is that if you can do this on the beach or hill, or even from your apartment window using a roof-top as a horizon, you'll be able to do it at sea. For some reason the movement of a boat bothers a sextant far less than it bothers a handbearing compass.

3 The noon sight for latitude

Local noon occurs at the moment when the Sun, on its journey from east to west, crosses the observer's meridian.

At any one time, you are on a particular terrestrial meridian of longitude. When the Sun bears exactly due south or due north of you, or once in a lifetime is right over your head (at your zenith), its celestial meridian (its GHA) will correspond to your longitude.

As we are about to see, if you can observe the altitude of any celestial body when it is exactly on your meridian, a very simple calculation will give you your latitude. Since finding your latitude is half the battle, and since the Sun is very much in evidence at noon, the noon sight has always been the cornerstone of the navigator's day.

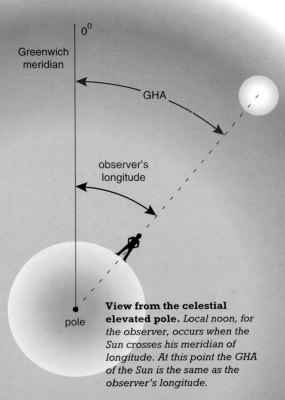

View from the celestial elevated pole. *Local noon, for the observer, occurs when the Sun crosses his meridian of longitude. At this point the GHA of the Sun is the same as the observer's longitude.*

FINDING THE TIME OF LOCAL NOON

Obviously the 'Greenwich' time of noon is going to vary from location to location as the Sun 'goes round the Earth'. When you are sitting on deck with your sextant you can tell when the Sun has reached its noon altitude because it doesn't get any higher.

Nevertheless you don't want to be hanging around all day waiting for it, so you need to be able to work out the approximate time of local noon.

Since the Sun completes its (apparent) journey once every 24 hours, and during that time traverses 360°, it follows that in one hour it will move through 15°, or one degree every four minutes.

The Sun is proceeding west from Greenwich, so if you are in west longitude, your local noon will be *later* than Greenwich, and if you are in east longitude, it will be *earlier*.

To determine how much earlier or later, simply multiply the number of degrees you are east or west of Greenwich by four: this gives you the number of minutes by which your local noon will differ from the time of noon at Greenwich. (There is an arc-to-time conversion table in the almanac that does this for you, if you prefer.)

Have a look at the daily page of the almanac illustrated on page 31, and at the bottom right-hand corner you will see a box labelled SUN and MOON. The column headed 'MER PASS' gives the time that the Sun will cross the Greenwich meridian on that day.

However unsure of your position you may be, you can always take a stab at a DR (dead reckoning) longitude for the time of local noon. Go for a whole degree and make sure you err on the 'early' side. You don't want to miss it.

Example 1

What time is local noon in DR longitude 4°W on May 2nd 1986?

Mer pass at Greenwich	11h 57m
4W W = +	16m
Local noon	12h 13m GMT

Example 2

What time is local noon in DR longitude 73°E on October 26th 1986?

Mer pass at Greenwich	11h 44m
73E E = —	4h 52m
Local noon	06h 52m GMT

If you happen to be sailing around within a few degrees of the Date Line on the opposite side of the globe from the Greenwich Meridian, a query may arise as to which day it is. If this is so, refer to Chapter 4, pages 25-6. If not, just remember that you have calculated the *Greenwich Time* of noon for your approximate longitude, and read on.

TAKING THE SIGHT

Once you know the approximate time of local noon, all that remains is to get up on deck 10 minutes or so early and start shooting the Sun's altitude.

You'll find it is still rising when you begin, but as it approaches its highest point you will be 'racking it down' slower and slower, until it stands still for a moment or two. That is the noon altitude. Whatever you do, don't start to rack the Sun up again as it begins to fall. Just wait until the lower limb bites positively into the horizon

without altering the sextant again and you know you have it. Noon is past and gone for another day. Note the log; go below, read your sextant, put it away and then work out your latitude.

THE THEORY

The illustration opposite demonstrates the noon sight set-up when viewed from the celestial elevated pole.

The illustration below shows it as seen from the celestial equator. Note how the celestial horizon makes a right-angle with the line dropped from the observer's zenith, through his geographic position to the centre of the Earth. *Zenith Distance* (ZD) is the only new concept to grab hold of. It is, quite simply, the angular distance (measured in degrees) between the observer's zenith and the position of the Sun on the celestial sphere.

Since the line from the observer's zenith meets the celestial horizon at 90°, the zenith distance must equal 90° minus the Sun's altitude:

$$ZD = 90° - ALTITUDE$$

You can see from the illustration below that latitude is the same angle on the terrestrial sphere as ZD + declination is on the celestial. Declination can be found in the almanac, and you can easily work out ZD.

Add them together, and that's your latitude - given that your latitude is greater than the Sun's declination, and of the same 'name' (i.e. north or

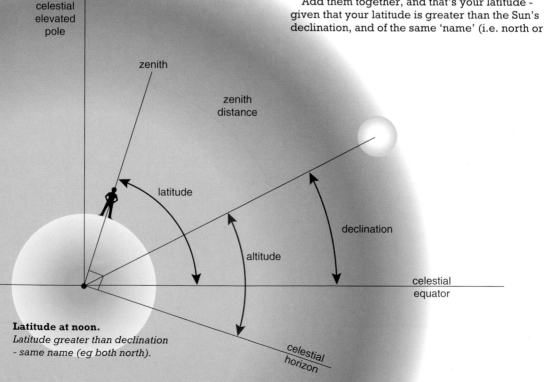

Latitude at noon.
Latitude greater than declination - same name (eg both north).

Latitude and declination with different names.

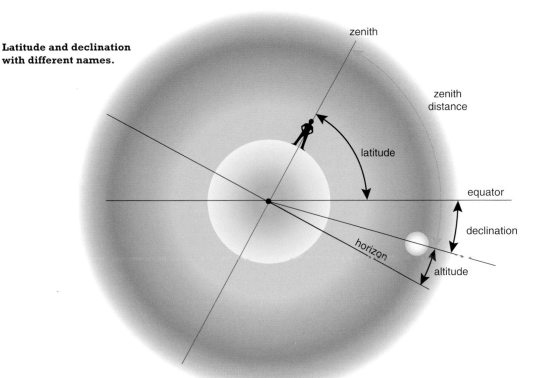

south), as it is in this case:

LAT = ZD + DEC

However, quite frequently, depending upon the season and where you are, latitude and declination will have different names and relative values. There are two other cases which may arise. In the diagram above, the latitude is the opposite 'name' to the declination and you can see that LAT = ZD — DEC.
The diagram opposite illustrates a situation that you meet in the tropics, where your latitude may be the same name as the declination, but could well be a lower value (e.g. latitude 12°N, Sun's declination 22°N). Here, LAT = DEC —ZD.

Spelled out in rote rule form, latitudes can be expressed as follows:

Latitude GREATER than declination. Same name:
LAT = ZD + DEC

Latitude OPPOSITE name to declination:
LAT = ZD — DEC

Latitude LESS than declination. Same name:
LAT = DEC — ZD

In practice, unless your voyage passes 'under'

the Sun or takes place during an equinox when the Sun's declination changes name, you'll have to make this decision only once per trip. The answer is the same every day.

So, to work a noon sight, what do you need?

- A *corrected* sextant altitude (Ho).
- The zenith distance (ZD = 90° — Ho).
- The declination of the Sun at the time of your sight (*not* at Greenwich noon, please!)
Insert ZD and DEC into one of the three formulae and...

YOU HAVE A LATITUDE

Example
2nd May 1986. Your DR is 50° 25′N 7°W. Local noon is therefore 1225 GMT. This enables you to obtain the declination of the Sun (DEC) from the almanac. Using the sextant, you find that the Sun's *corrected* altitude (Ho) at noon is 54° 47′.4. What is your latitude?

LAT = ZD + DEC

Dec 12h	N 15° 22′ .4
+ 25m ('d' = + 0.7)	0′ .3
Dec 1225	N 15° 22′ .7

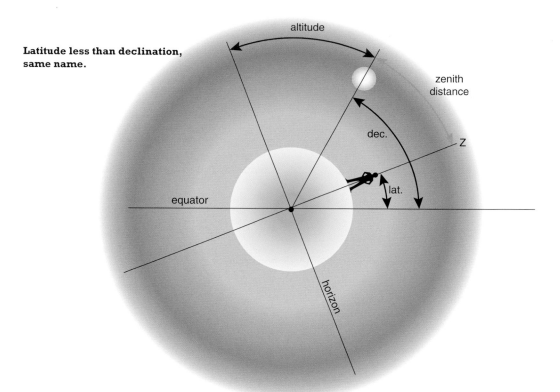

Latitude less than declination, same name.

altitude

zenith distance

dec.

Z

equator

lat.

horizon

90	89°	60′	
— Ho	54°	47′	.4
= ZD	35°	12′	.6
+ Dec	N 15°	22′	.7
Lat	N 50°	35′	.3

(* To make the subtraction easier I always express 90° as 89° 60′. It gives you less figures to carry.)

OTHER BODIES

The theory of working out a latitude from a body on your meridian holds good for everything in the sky, not just the Sun. The Sun is the most popular, though, because it is on the meridian at noon and can be employed in conjunction with a forenoon sight (see Chapter 6) to produce a fix, but don't discount the possibility of using a suitable star at twilight, a planet, or the Moon. A latitude is a very useful thing to have.

'MAXIMUM' ALTITUDES

In theory, the system described above for determining latitude works perfectly only from a stationary vessel, or one which is travelling exactly east or west. The reason is that if you are in the northern hemisphere and sailing southwards towards the Sun (your latitude being greater than its declination), your changing latitude will cause the Sun to continue to 'rise' while it is actually past your meridian. Similarly if you were moving in a northerly direction, the Sun's altitude would begin to decrease before it reached your meridian.

For a fast-moving ship doing 20 knots or so due north or south, this can produce errors of up to five minutes of arc. In a sailing yacht working manfully to keep up her five knots it is rarely a factor to consider. However, if you have a big north/south component in your course, bear in mind that your latitude from a meridian sight may not be quite as accurate as you would hope.

Allowing for the maximum altitude effect

Since the Sun is crossing the meridians at the rate of one every four minutes you should, unless your DR is wildly astray, be able to work out to the nearest minute or so the time that the Sun will pass the meridian of your noon DR longitude.

Take the Sun's altitude at about this time instead of waiting for it to reach its highest point, and that will be as near to the meridian altitude as you are going to get. Remember that, this close to noon, if the altitude is changing at all, it will be changing very slowly.

4 Time

In Chapter 3, while considering the Greenwich time of local noon for our longitude, we looked at the basic relationship of arc and time, and found it to be:

ONE DAY = 360°
ONE HOUR = 360° ÷ 24 = 15°
FOUR MINUTES = 1°

However, whereas a degree can be defined as 1/360 of a circle, the definition of a day is not quite so clear-cut. This is because, amongst other things, the Earth is travelling in its orbit round the Sun at the same time as it revolves, and orbits are sometimes a little less regular than the mathematicians would desire.

A suitable definition of a day might be the time taken for the Sun to proceed from our nadir (midnight) through sunrise, across our meridian, down through sunset and back to our nadir once more. Unfortunately, when measured in hours this does not take exactly the same amount of time on every occasion, so to make life tolerable for us all, we must compute an average time for it.

Since the celestial co-ordinates for every day are tabulated in one nautical almanac it was decided long ago to refer them all to the average (or *mean*) time as measured at the Greenwich Observatory, England, giving us our old friend Greenwich Mean Time (GMT).

THE 'MEAN SUN' AND THE 'APPARENT SUN'

The *mean* Sun is the imaginary body moving with perfect regularity from which GMT is taken. It represents an average of the motions of the *true* or *apparent* Sun (both words have the same meaning in this instance). The mean Sun and the apparent Sun are frequently well adrift from one another.

The difference between the two is called the equation of time and is to be found in the same box as the time of the Sun's meridian passage in the daily pages of the almanac. If, for example, the Sun were 1° 30' East of Greenwich at noon GMT, this equation of time would be six minutes.

Although this figure is seldom used in practice, the fact that there is a difference between the mean and apparent Sun makes it important to check the actual time of the Sun's meridian passage (i.e. apparent noon) each day before deciding when to take your noon sight.

ZONE TIME

Navigators and astronomers may be content to live their lives by GMT, but the general public spoil all that by insisting on lunching at 1300 hours, no matter where they are, and expecting the Sun to rise at 0600. They set their clocks by the movement of the Sun and, in consequence, 'working time' alters from place to place around the globe.

In fact, the time of sunrise, say, varies with every step you take east or west, but if each town and village worked to its own time the result would be chaos. In order to simplify this business the world is divided into 24 *time zones*. Not surprisingly, each time zone is 15° of longitude across.

Each meridian divisible by 15 is a *zone meridian* and its time zone spreads out 7½° to either side of it.

NAMING THE ZONES: '+' or '—'

Since the Sun rises in the east and proceeds to the westward across the sky it follows that it will rise later in 90°W than it does at Greenwich. Actually it will rise 90÷15, or six hours later. So when the Sun is rising at 0600 at Greenwich, it is midnight (0000 hours) in Chicago at 90°W.

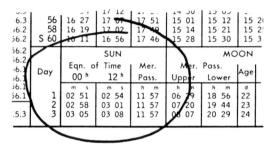

6.3	56	16 27	17 07	17 51	15 01	15 12	15 20
.6.2	58	16 19	17 02	17 49	15 14	15 21	15 2
56.2	S 60	16 11	16 56	17 46	15 28	15 30	15 3

		SUN			MOON		
	Day	Eqn. of Time		Mer.	Mer. Pass.		Age
		00 h	12 h	Pass.	Upper	Lower	
56.1		m s	m s	h m	h m	h m	d
56.1	1	02 51	02 54	11 57	06 29	18 56	22
	2	02 58	03 01	11 57	07 20	19 44	23
.5.3	3	03 05	03 08	11 57	08 07	20 29	24

The actual time of the Sun's meridian passage, and the difference between this and noon GMT, is given in the daily pages of the almanac.

0600 GMT

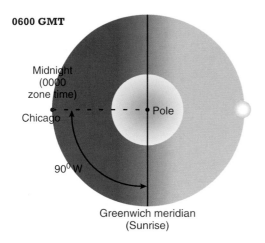

Greenwich meridian
(Sunrise)

1200 GMT

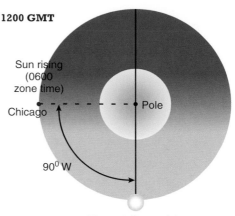

Noon at Greenwich
(Sun on meridian)

Six hours later, when the Sun does rise in Chicago, the time there will be, conveniently, 0600 hours.

By then it will be 1200 (noon) at Greenwich and nearly time for lunch.

At any given instant, if you have your watch set to Chicago time and you want to convert it to Greenwich, you'll have to *add* six hours. Chicago is therefore said to be in 'Zone + 6'. In the same way, all the western time zones, right round to the International Date Line, are named 'plus'.

All the eastern time zones are named 'minus'. The Sun rises in, say, Moscow before it does at Greenwich, so zone time at Moscow will be later than Greenwich and you'll have to subtract the relevant number of hours to reduce Moscow time to Greenwich time.

The divisions between time zones, for reasons of national convenience, do not always fall exactly halfway between the zone meridians concerned. France, for example, in order to fit in with the rest of continental Europe, has placed itself in 'Zone - 1', although most of its land mass falls plumb into the Greenwich time zone.

This sort of thing won't affect your ship's working clock in mid-ocean, but it is as well to be aware of it. Tide tables, for example, are usually issued in the official zone time of the country concerned, regardless of its longitude.

A few examples

Since all tabulated celestial data refer to GMT, you will constantly be converting from your ship's zone time to Greenwich time and vice versa. Once again, practice makes it easy, but in the meantime here are some examples to clarify the matter:

Q What time zone are you in if your longitude is 170°W?
A Zone + 11.
Q What will your ship's clock say at 1000 GMT in 10°E longitude?
A 10°E is Zone - 1. This means that you must subtract one hour from your zone time to get down to Greenwich, so your zone time must be 1100.
Q Which meridian will you have crossed on a westbound passage of the north Atlantic when the ship's clock goes back from GMT - 3 to GMT - 4? (Remember that in west longitude, you are in Zone + 3 and moving to Zone + 4 as you move away from Greenwich. At any time you must add time to your zone time to get up to Greenwich, so your ship's clock will show an earlier time than Greenwich. Remember that the man in Chicago was getting up when the Greenwich observer sat down to his lunch.)
A The zone meridian for Zone + 3 is 3 x 15° = 45°W.
The zone meridian for Zone + 4 is 4 x 15° = 60°W.
Halfway between the two you change zones, so the boundary between Zone + 3 and Zone + 4 falls at 52½°W. (See diagram page 26.)

Change of date and the International Date Line

Watch out for this one. If it arises, tackle it logically and it will present no problem. Let us assume you are in Zone + 8. It is 1830 zone time (ZT) on March 25th. What is GMT? If you are in Zone + 8, you will add eight hours to 1830 ZT and come up with 2630 GMT on March 25th. Obviously this means 0230 GMT on March 26th. That's better.

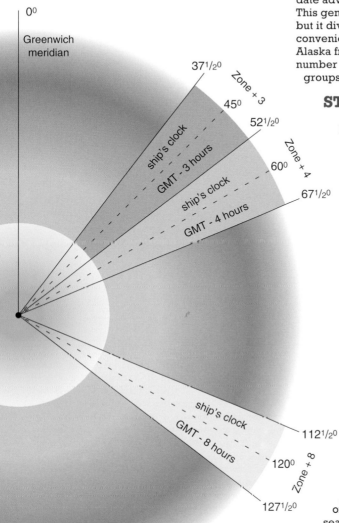

date advances for ease of administration. This generally follows the 180th meridian, but it diverts here and there for the sake of convenience. The zig-zag which separates Alaska from Siberia is a case in point, as are a number of kinks which keep Pacific island groups together.

STANDARD TIME

In order to make best use of the local electricity supplies by extending daylight into the evenings, many countries choose to add one hour (or even two hours) to their zone time during the summer.

These arrangements are purely domestic and have no relevance to the astro-navigator, but if you are setting sail on a voyage from a country operating such an arrangement, don't forget to set your ship's clock to something more sensible as soon as you leave, or you may have a debacle.

It's also important to be aware of standard time when you arrive or you may be caught out by that greatest of disasters: to step ashore after crossing an ocean only to discover that the pubs have just shut.

THE NAVIGATION CLOCK

Just in case you have a mental block on questions of time when you are at sea, all problems can be solved by referring to your navigation clock, which you should keep set on GMT. Even if you actually time your sights with your quartz wristwatch, as I do, you should always have a back-up clock somewhere on board. Personally I keep my wristwatch on zone time, which on my boat is usually ship's time, but if my mind blows a fuse while thrashing to windward when I am dog tired, I can always refer to the navigation clock to check up on GMT.

While this arrangement will stand you in good stead for navigational purposes, it does not do to forget the International Date Line which runs north-south from pole to pole and where the

5 Position lines and plotting

As with coastal navigation, a position obtained using astro-navigation techniques is plotted on a chart using position lines (PLs), but instead of being straight, these are (theoretically) circular. Most of the position lines used in coastal navigation are straight lines, but there are one or two sources of PL, generally thought of as methods of determining 'distance off', which are in fact circular lines of position.

around it and know that we would be somewhere on that circle.

In astro-navigation, all the PLs are actually parts of a circle scribed around the geographic position (on the terrestrial sphere) of the body observed, but the circles are so huge that a short section of the circle looks like a straight line.

AZIMUTH

For such a huge circle to be usable you need to know which section of it to draw on your chart. To determine this you employ a line which gives the bearing of the body from your rough position (in degrees True) and then construct your PL at right angles to it. This 'bearing line' is called an azimuth (Zn) and is defined as 'the

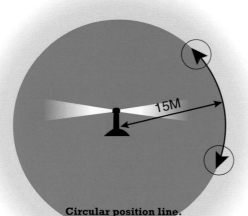

Circular position line.
If you know your distance from a lighthouse but you have no compass, you know that you are somewhere on a circular position line

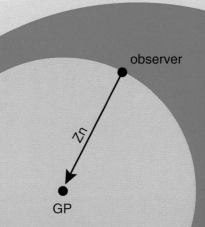

If you know the altitude of a star, you can locate yourself on a circle of position because the altitude of the star will be the same from any point on the circle. The azimuth (Zn) is a bearing to the geographic posiiton (GP) that tells you which part of the circle to use.

circle of position

Consider, for example, the 'rising' or 'dipping' lighthouse. The tables tell us that with a height of eye of eight feet we will see such and such a light 'rise' at a distance of 15 miles. When it pops up we dutifully take a magnetic bearing and mark off our position 15 miles out from the lighthouse. If we didn't have any means of determining the bearing of the light, however, we would be left with just the knowledge that we were 15 miles from it. We could scribe a circle 15 miles in radius

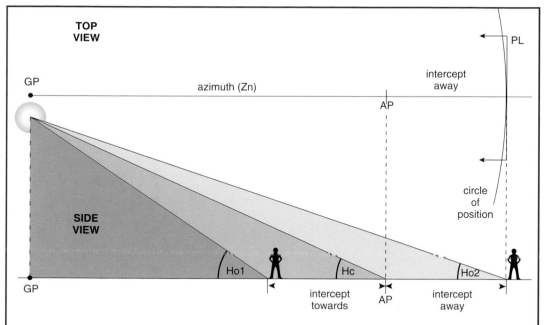

The side view shows how the difference between observed altitude (Ho) and calculated altitude (Hc) is used to find the direction of the intercept from the assumed position (AP). If Ho is less than Hc, for example, the intercept is away from the celestial body, as shown in the top view. Notice that the PL is actually at a tangent to the circle of position.

horizontal direction of a celestial point from a terrestrial point'. (Incidentally, the word is pronounced 'azzmuth'.)

To work up a PL, first calculate what the altitude and azimuth of the body would be at the time of your sight from a convenient assumed position (AP). This should be as close as possible to where you think you are (your DR position), but is rarely the same. This is because the AP is selected to fit in with the information in the almanac and sight reduction tables which is presented in convenient 'steps' of whole degrees. The technique of calculating the altitude and azimuth of the body from the AP is described in Chapter 6.

Because the distances from both your DR and AP to the geographic position of the body are so enormous, the azimuth to either position can be considered to be the same. The altitude that you have observed using your sextant, however, is usually different from the one you have calculated from your assumed position. This difference, which is measured in minutes of arc, is called the *intercept* and can be expressed on the chart as minutes of latitude, or nautical miles. In effect, your AP is functioning as a datum, and the intercept gives you the distance from this

datum to your position line.

In the diagram above you can see what all this actually means. You will notice that if the observed altitude from your actual position (Ho) is greater than the calculated altitude at the

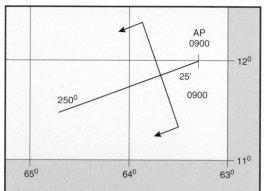

A position line (PL) plotted on a chart. The azimuth has been drawn in at 250° from the AP, and the PL drawn across it at right angles 25' from the AP towards the body.

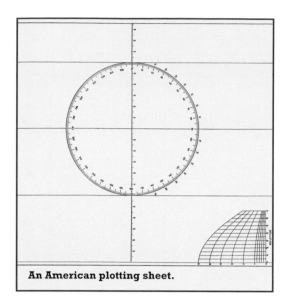

An American plotting sheet.

1 Mark the assumed position (AP).
2 Draw the azimuth (Zn) passing through it.
3 Decide whether the intercept is towards or away from the body. In this case it is towards. The Zn is 250° which means that the body bears 250° from the AP, so you measure off the intercept in that direction.
4 Construct your PL, which will pass through the intercept at right angles to the azimuth. The PL is marked as a straight line with arrowheads at each end pointing towards the body.

Note: The point at which the PL crosses the azimuth is NOT A FIX. It is merely a reference point from which to construct your PL, which has much the same function as a bearing line from an observed object such as a buoy. To achieve a fix you need at least one more PL. More about this later.

Plotting charts

If you are sailing in coastal waters you can usually plot your sights directly onto your working chart. In mid-ocean, however, the scale of the chart makes accurate plotting impossible. Instead, use a plotting chart.

These can be made up yourself, but they are so cheap to buy that I always kit up with a sheaf before I set sail. They are recyclable, so don't worry about having enough to last the voyage. Plotting charts come in various forms with a variety of scales. I prefer those issued by the United States Defense Mapping Agency. The scale is realistic and with careful use of a sharp pencil a whole day's run can be fitted onto one chart.

The illustration shows a blank of this form. To use it designate one of the transverse lines as your assumed latitude and then take measurements for your assumed longitude from the scale at the bottom right-hand corner. All further measurements of intercept, etc., are marked off utilising the latitude scale printed down the middle of the sheet.

The compass rose is there purely for the convenience of those plotting with parallel rulers. Personally I always use a Douglas (square) Protractor for plotting astro PLs. Once you have fixed your position on the plotting chart, you can express it in terms of latitude and longitude, log it and transfer it to your ocean chart.

assumed position (Hc), then the PL will be nearer to the geographic position (GP) of the body. Conversely, if the Ho is less than the Hc, the PL will be further away.

Because the assumed position is effectively on the same azimuth as your actual position you never need to know what the GP of the body really is. You simply draw a short section of the azimuth through the assumed position on your chart. Then, if the Ho is *greater* than the Hc, you mark off your intercept so many miles *in the direction* of the body. If the Ho is less than the Hc, mark it off *away* from it. Then you draw your PL through your intercept, at right angles to the azimuth.

The rule to remember for which way to mark off your intercept is this:

Calculated **(Tabulated)** altitude less **(Tinier)** than observed altitude: intercept **Towards** the body.
Tabulated; Tinier; Towards - TTT

Clearly, if the Ho is less than the Hc the converse will apply. Intercepts are always labelled 'towards' or 'away'.

PRACTICAL PLOTTING

Illustrated above is a section of a chart. In order to plot a sight all you have to do is:

1986 MAY 1, 2, 3 (THURS., FRI., SAT.)

G.M.T. (UT)	ARIES G.H.A.	VENUS −3.3 G.H.A.	Dec.	MARS −0.5 G.H.A.	Dec.	JUPITER −1.7 G.H.A.	Dec.	SATURN +0.3 G.H.A.	Dec.	STARS Name	S.H.A.	Dec.
1 00	218 37.7	155 34.7	N21 49.4	292 06.7	S23 43.5	231 43.9	S 6 40.4	331 44.2	S19 41.3	Acamar	315 34.3	S40 21.6
01	233 40.2	170 34.0	50.1	307 08.1	43.5	246 46.0	40.3	346 46.8	41.3	Achernar	335 42.4	S57 18.3
02	248 42.6	185 33.3	50.7	322 09.6	43.5	261 48.0	40.1	1 49.5	41.3	Acrux	173 32.3	S63 01.6
03	263 45.1	200 32.5	·· 51.4	337 11.0	·· 43.5	276 50.0	·· 39.9	16 52.1	·· 41.3	Adhara	255 29.0	S28 57.3
04	278 47.5	215 31.8	52.0	352 12.5	43.5	291 52.0	39.8	31 54.7	41.2	Aldebaran	291 13.5	N16 29.0
05	293 50.0	230 31.0	52.7	7 14.0	43.5	306 54.1	39.6	46 57.3	41.2			
06	308 52.5	245 30.3	N21 53.3	22 15.4	S23 43.5	321 56.1	S 6 39.4	62 00.0	S19 41.2	Alioth	166 38.0	N56 02.1
07	323 54.9	260 29.6	54.0	37 16.9	43.5	336 58.1	39.2	77 02.6	41.2	Alkaid	153 14.5	N49 22.9
T 08	338 57.4	275 28.8	54.6	52 18.3	43.5	352 00.2	39.1	92 05.2	41.1	Al Na'ir	28 09.6	S47 01.6
H 09	353 59.9	290 28.1	·· 55.3	67 19.8	·· 43.5	7 02.2	·· 38.9	107 07.8	·· 41.1	Alnilam	276 07.6	S 1 12.6
U 10	9 02.3	305 27.3	55.9	82 21.3	43.5	22 04.2	38.7	122 10.4	41.1	Alphard	218 16.4	S 8 36.0
R 11	24 04.8	320 26.6	56.6	97 22.7	43.5	37 06.3	38.6	137 13.1	41.1			
S 12	39 07.3	335 25.9	N21 57.2	112 24.2	S23 43.6	52 08.3	S 6 38.4	152 15.7	S19 41.0	Alphecca	126 28.1	N26 45.4
D 13	54 09.7	350 25.1	57.9	127 25.7	43.6	67 10.4	38.2	167 18.3	41.0	Alpheratz	358 05.3	N29 00.7
A 14	69 12.2	5 24.4	58.5	142 27.1	43.6	82 12.4	38.0	182 20.9	41.0	Altair	62 28.3	N 8 49.6
Y 15	84 14.7	20 23.6	·· 59.1	157 28.6	·· 43.6	97 14.4	·· 37.9	197 23.6	·· 41.0	Ankaa	353 36.2	S42 22.8
16	99 17.1	35 22.9	21 59.8	172 30.1	43.6	112 16.5	37.7	212 26.2	40.9	Antares	112 51.4	S26 24.3
17	114 19.6	50 22.1	22 00.4	187 31.5	43.6	127 18.5	37.5	227 28.8	40.9			
18	129 22.0	65 21.4	N22 01.1	202 33.0	S23 43.6	142 20.5	S 6 37.4	242 31.4	S19 40.9	Arcturus	146 14.2	N19 15.1
19	144 24.5	80 20.7	01.7	217 34.5	43.6	157 22.6	37.2	257 34.1	40.8	Atria	108 11.5	S69 00.2
20	159 27.0	95 19.9	02.3	232 35.9	43.6	172 24.6	37.0	272 36.7	40.8	Avior	234 26.8	S59 28.1
21	174 29.4	110 19.2	·· 03.0	247 37.4	·· 43.6	187 26.6	·· 36.9	287 39.3	·· 40.8	Bellatrix	278 54.5	N 6 20.3
22	189 31.9	125 18.4	03.6	262 38.9	43.6	202 28.7	36.7	302 41.9	40.8	Betelgeuse	271 23.9	N 7 24.4
23	204 34.4	140 17.7	04.2	277 40.3	43.6	217 30.7	36.5	317 44.6	40.7			
2 00	219 36.8	155 16.9	N22 04.9	292 41.8	S23 43.6	232 32.7	S 6 36.3	332 47.2	S19 40.7	Canopus	264 05.7	S52 41.4
01	234 39.3	170 16.2	05.5	307 43.3	43.6	247 34.8	36.2	347 49.8	40.7	Capella	281 05.5	N45 59.3
02	249 41.8	185 15.4	06.1	322 44.8	43.6	262 36.8	36.0	2 52.5	40.7	Deneb	49 45.7	N45 13.4
03	264 44.2	200 14.7	·· 06.8	337 46.2	·· 43.6	277 38.8	·· 35.8	17 55.1	·· 40.6	Denebola	182 54.4	N14 38.9
04	279 46.7	215 13.9	07.4	352 47.7	43.6	292 40.9	35.7	32 57.7	40.6	Diphda	349 16.8	S18 03.8
05	294 49.2	230 13.2	08.0	7 49.2	43.6	307 42.9	35.5	48 00.3	40.6			
06	309 51.6	245 12.4	N22 08.6	22 50.6	S23 43.6	322 45.0	S 6 35.3	63 03.0	S19 40.6	Dubhe	194 16.2	N61 49.8
07	324 54.1	260 11.7	09.3	37 52.1	43.6	337 47.0	35.2	78 05.6	40.5	Elnath	278 39.1	N28 35.9
08	339 56.5	275 10.9	09.9	52 53.6	43.6	352 49.0	35.0	93 08.2	40.5	Eltanin	90 55.4	N51 29.2
F 09	354 59.0	290 10.2	·· 10.5	67 55.1	·· 43.6	7 51.1	·· 34.8	108 10.8	·· 40.5	Enif	34 07.5	N 9 48.4
R 10	10 01.5	305 09.4	11.1	82 56.6	43.7	22 53.1	34.6	123 13.5	40.5	Fomalhaut	15 46.8	S29 41.7
I 11	25 03.9	320 08.7	11.8	97 58.0	43.7	37 55.1	34.5	138 16.1	40.4			
D 12	40 06.4	335 07.9	N22 12.4	112 59.5	S23 43.7	52 57.2	S 6 34.3	153 18.7	S19 40.4	Gacrux	172 23.9	S57 02.4
A 13	55 08.9	350 07.2	13.0	128 01.0	43.7	67 59.2	34.1	168 21.3	40.4	Gienah	176 13.4	S17 28.1
Y 14	70 11.3	5 06.4	13.6	143 02.5	43.7	83 01.3	34.0	183 24.0	40.4	Hadar	149 17.0	S60 18.6
15	85 13.8	20 05.7	·· 14.2	158 04.0	·· 43.7	98 03.3	·· 33.8	198 26.6	·· 40.3	Hamal	328 24.6	N23 23.8
16	100 16.3	35 04.9	14.8	173 05.4	43.7	113 05.3	33.6	213 29.2	40.3	Kaus Aust.	84 11.0	S34 23.6
17	115 18.7	50 04.2	15.5	188 06.9	43.7	128 07.4	33.5	228 31.9	40.3			
18	130 21.2	65 03.4	N22 16.1	203 08.4	S23 43.7	143 09.4	S 6 33.3	243 34.5	S19 40.2	Kochab	137 17.4	N74 12.6
19	145 23.6	80 02.7	16.7	218 09.9	43.7	158 11.5	33.1	258 37.1	40.2	Markab	13 59.2	N15 07.6
20	160 26.1	95 01.9	17.3	233 11.4	43.7	173 13.5	33.0	273 39.7	40.2	Menkar	314 37.0	N 4 02.2
21	175 28.6	110 01.2	·· 17.9	248 12.9	·· 43.7	188 15.5	·· 32.8	288 42.4	·· 40.2	Menkent	148 31.8	S36 18.3
22	190 31.0	125 00.4	18.5	263 14.4	43.7	203 17.6	32.6	303 45.0	40.1	Miaplacidus	221 44.4	S69 39.9
23	205 33.5	139 59.6	19.1	278 15.8	43.7	218 19.6	32.4	318 47.6	40.1			
3 00	220 36.0	154 58.9	N22 19.7	293 17.3	S23 43.7	233 21.7	S 6 32.3	333 50.2	S19 40.1	Mirfak	309 10.7	N49 48.8
01	235 38.4	169 58.1	20.3	308 18.8	43.7	248 23.7	32.1	348 52.9	40.1	Nunki	76 23.7	S26 19.0
02	250 40.9	184 57.4	20.9	323 20.3	43.7	263 25.7	31.9	3 55.5	40.0	Peacock	53 51.4	S56 46.7
03	265 43.4	199 56.6	·· 21.5	338 21.8	·· 43.7	278 27.8	·· 31.8	18 58.1	·· 40.0	Pollux	243 53.1	N28 03.8
04	280 45.8	214 55.9	22.1	353 23.3	43.8	293 29.8	31.6	34 00.8	40.0	Procyon	245 21.5	N 5 15.7
05	295 48.3	229 55.1	22.7	8 24.8	43.8	308 31.9	31.4	49 03.4	40.0			
06	310 50.8	244 54.3	N22 23.3	23 26.3	S23 43.8	323 33.9	S 6 31.3	64 06.0	S19 39.9	Rasalhague	96 25.4	N12 33.9
07	325 53.2	259 53.6	23.9	38 27.8	43.8	338 35.9	31.1	79 08.6	39.9	Regulus	208 05.4	N12 02.1
S 08	340 55.7	274 52.8	24.5	53 29.3	43.8	353 38.0	30.9	94 11.3	39.9	Rigel	281 32.2	S 8 13.0
A 09	355 58.1	289 52.1	·· 25.1	68 30.8	·· 43.8	8 40.0	·· 30.8	109 13.9	·· 39.9	Rigil Kent.	140 19.7	S60 46.8
T 10	11 00.6	304 51.3	25.7	83 32.3	43.8	23 42.1	30.6	124 16.5	39.8	Sabik	102 36.0	S15 42.7
U 11	26 03.1	319 50.5	26.3	98 33.8	43.8	38 44.1	30.4	139 19.2	39.8			
R 12	41 05.5	334 49.8	N22 26.9	113 35.2	S23 43.8	53 46.1	S 6 30.3	154 21.8	S19 39.8	Schedar	350 05.0	N56 27.5
D 13	56 08.0	349 49.0	27.5	128 36.7	43.8	68 48.2	30.1	169 24.4	39.7	Shaula	96 49.7	S37 05.8
A 14	71 10.5	4 48.3	28.1	143 38.2	43.8	83 50.2	29.9	184 27.1	39.7	Sirius	258 52.1	S16 41.9
Y 15	86 12.9	19 47.5	·· 28.7	158 39.7	·· 43.8	98 52.3	·· 29.8	199 29.7	·· 39.7	Spica	158 52.8	S11 05.5
16	101 15.4	34 46.7	29.3	173 41.2	43.8	113 54.3	29.6	214 32.3	39.7	Suhail	223 07.8	S43 22.8
17	116 17.9	49 46.0	29.9	188 42.7	43.8	128 56.4	29.4	229 34.9	39.6			
18	131 20.3	64 45.2	N22 30.5	203 44.2	S23 43.8	143 58.4	S 6 29.3	244 37.6	S19 39.6	Vega	80 52.8	N38 45.8
19	146 22.8	79 44.5	31.0	218 45.7	43.9	159 00.4	29.1	259 40.2	39.6	Zuben'ubi	137 28.1	S15 59.3
20	161 25.3	94 43.7	31.6	233 47.3	43.9	174 02.5	28.9	274 42.8	39.6		S.H.A.	Mer. Pass.
21	176 27.7	109 42.9	·· 32.2	248 48.8	·· 43.9	189 04.5	·· 28.8	289 45.5	39.5			h m
22	191 30.2	124 42.2	32.8	263 50.3	43.9	204 06.6	28.6	304 48.1	39.5	Venus	295 40.1	13 40
23	206 32.6	139 41.4	33.4	278 51.8	43.9	219 08.6	28.4	319 50.7	39.5	Mars	73 05.0	4 29
Mer. Pass.	h m 9 20.0	v −0.8	d 0.6	v 1.5	d 0.0	v 2.0	d 0.2	v 2.6	d 0.0	Jupiter	12 55.9	8 29
										Saturn	113 10.4	1 49

Table 1. Daily Page from The Nautical Almanac..

1986 MAY 1, 2, 3 (THURS., FRI., SAT.)

SUN and MOON

G.M.T. (UT) d h	SUN G.H.A.	SUN Dec.	MOON G.H.A.	v	MOON Dec.	d	H.P.
1 00	180 42.7	N14 55.3	266 09.8	08.1	S23 09.8	09.7	58.1
01	195 42.8	56.0	280 36.9	08.1	23 00.1	09.8	58.1
02	210 42.9	56.8	295 04.0	08.3	22 50.3	09.9	58.1
03	225 42.9	.. 57.6	309 31.3	08.4	22 40.4	10.0	58.0
04	240 43.0	58.3	323 58.7	08.6	22 30.4	10.2	58.0
05	255 43.1	59.1	338 26.3	08.7	22 20.2	10.3	58.0
06	270 43.2	N14 59.9	352 54.0	08.7	S22 09.9	10.3	57.9
07	285 43.3	15 00.6	7 21.7	09.0	21 59.6	10.5	57.9
T 08	300 43.3	01.4	21 49.7	09.0	21 49.1	10.6	57.9
H 09	315 43.4	.. 02.1	36 17.7	09.2	21 38.5	10.7	57.8
U 10	330 43.5	02.9	50 45.9	09.2	21 27.8	10.8	57.8
R 11	345 43.6	03.6	65 14.1	09.5	21 17.0	10.9	57.8
S 12	0 43.6	N15 04.4	79 42.6	09.5	S21 06.1	11.0	57.7
D 13	15 43.7	05.2	94 11.1	09.6	20 55.1	11.1	57.7
A 14	30 43.8	05.9	108 39.7	09.8	20 44.0	11.3	57.7
Y 15	45 43.9	.. 06.7	123 08.5	09.9	20 32.7	11.3	57.6
16	60 43.9	07.4	137 37.4	10.0	20 21.4	11.4	57.6
17	75 44.0	08.2	152 06.4	10.1	20 10.0	11.4	57.6
18	90 44.1	N15 08.9	166 35.5	10.2	S19 58.6	11.6	57.6
19	105 44.2	09.7	181 04.7	10.4	19 47.0	11.7	57.5
20	120 44.2	10.4	195 34.1	10.4	19 35.3	11.7	57.5
21	135 44.3	.. 11.2	210 03.5	10.6	19 23.6	11.9	57.5
22	150 44.4	11.9	224 33.1	10.7	19 11.7	11.9	57.4
23	165 44.5	12.7	239 02.8	10.8	18 59.8	12.0	57.4
2 00	180 44.5	N15 13.4	253 32.6	11.0	S18 47.8	12.1	57.4
01	195 44.6	14.2	268 02.6	11.0	18 35.7	12.2	57.3
02	210 44.7	14.9	282 32.6	11.1	18 23.5	12.2	57.3
03	225 44.8	.. 15.7	297 02.7	11.3	18 11.3	12.4	57.3
04	240 44.8	16.4	311 33.0	11.3	17 58.9	12.4	57.2
05	255 44.9	17.2	326 03.3	11.5	17 46.5	12.5	57.2
06	270 45.0	N15 17.9	340 33.8	11.6	S17 34.0	12.5	57.2
07	285 45.1	18.7	355 04.4	11.7	17 21.5	12.6	57.1
08	300 45.1	19.4	9 35.1	11.7	17 08.9	12.7	57.1
F 09	315 45.2	.. 20.2	24 05.8	11.9	16 56.2	12.8	57.1
R 10	330 45.3	20.9	38 36.7	12.0	16 43.4	12.8	57.1
I 11	345 45.3	21.7	53 07.7	12.1	16 30.6	12.9	57.0
D 12	0 45.4	N15 22.4	67 38.8	12.2	S16 17.7	13.0	57.0
A 13	15 45.5	23.2	82 10.0	12.3	16 04.7	13.0	57.0
Y 14	30 45.5	23.9	96 41.3	12.4	15 51.7	13.1	56.9
15	45 45.6	.. 24.7	111 12.7	12.4	15 38.6	13.1	56.9
16	60 45.7	25.4	125 44.1	12.6	15 25.5	13.2	56.9
17	75 45.8	26.2	140 15.7	12.7	15 12.3	13.3	56.9
18	90 45.8	N15 26.9	154 47.4	12.7	S14 59.0	13.3	56.8
19	105 45.9	27.6	169 19.1	12.9	14 45.7	13.3	56.8
20	120 46.0	28.4	183 51.0	12.9	14 32.4	13.5	56.8
21	135 46.0	.. 29.1	198 22.9	13.1	14 18.9	13.4	56.7
22	150 46.1	29.9	212 55.0	13.1	14 05.5	13.6	56.7
23	165 46.2	30.6	227 27.1	13.2	13 51.9	13.5	56.7
3 00	180 46.2	N15 31.4	241 59.3	13.3	S13 38.4	13.7	56.7
01	195 46.3	32.1	256 31.6	13.4	13 24.7	13.6	56.6
02	210 46.4	32.8	271 04.0	13.5	13 11.1	13.8	56.6
03	225 46.4	.. 33.6	285 36.5	13.5	12 57.4	13.8	56.6
04	240 46.5	34.3	300 09.0	13.6	12 43.6	13.8	56.5
05	255 46.6	35.0	314 41.6	13.8	12 29.8	13.8	56.5
06	270 46.6	N15 35.8	329 14.4	13.7	S12 16.0	13.9	56.5
07	285 46.7	36.5	343 47.1	13.9	12 02.1	13.9	56.5
S 08	300 46.8	37.3	358 20.0	13.9	11 48.2	14.0	56.4
A 09	315 46.8	.. 38.0	12 52.9	14.1	11 34.2	14.0	56.4
T 10	330 46.9	38.7	27 26.0	14.1	11 20.2	14.0	56.4
U 11	345 47.0	39.5	41 59.1	14.1	11 06.2	14.1	56.4
R 12	0 47.0	N15 40.2	56 32.2	14.3	S10 52.1	14.1	56.3
D 13	15 47.1	40.9	71 05.5	14.3	10 38.0	14.2	56.3
A 14	30 47.2	41.7	85 38.8	14.3	10 23.8	14.1	56.3
Y 15	45 47.2	.. 42.4	100 12.1	14.5	10 09.7	14.2	56.3
16	60 47.3	43.1	114 45.6	14.5	9 55.5	14.3	56.2
17	75 47.3	43.9	129 19.1	14.5	9 41.2	14.2	56.2
18	90 47.4	N15 44.6	143 52.6	14.7	S 9 27.0	14.3	56.2
19	105 47.5	45.3	158 26.3	14.7	9 12.7	14.3	56.2
20	120 47.5	46.1	173 00.0	14.7	8 58.4	14.3	56.1
21	135 47.6	.. 46.8	187 33.7	14.9	8 44.1	14.4	56.1
22	150 47.6	47.5	202 07.6	14.8	8 29.7	14.4	56.1
23	165 47.7	48.3	216 41.4	15.0	8 15.3	14.4	56.1
	S.D. 15.9	d 0.7	S.D. 15.7		15.5		15.3

Twilight, Sunrise and Moonrise

Lat.	Twilight Naut.	Civil	Sunrise	Moonrise 1	2	3	4
N 72	////	////	01 47	■	06 28	04 56	04 13
N 70	////	00 59	02 27	■	05 25	04 34	04 03
68	////	01 51	02 54	■	04 49	04 17	03 55
66	////	02 09	03 15	04 59	04 23	04 03	03 48
64	////	02 27	03 31	04 19	04 02	03 51	03 42
62	00 52	02 45	03 45	03 51	03 46	03 41	03 37
60	01 39	03 03	03 56	03 29	03 32	03 33	03 32
N 58	02 07	03 17	04 06	03 11	03 20	03 25	03 28
56	02 28	03 30	04 15	02 56	03 10	03 18	03 25
54	02 45	03 41	04 22	02 43	03 00	03 12	03 22
52	03 00	03 50	04 29	02 32	02 52	03 07	03 19
50	03 12	03 59	04 35	02 22	02 45	03 02	03 16
45	03 36	04 16	04 48	02 00	02 29	02 51	03 10
N 40	03 54	04 30	04 59	01 43	02 16	02 42	03 05
35	04 09	04 41	05 09	01 28	02 04	02 35	03 01
30	04 21	04 51	05 17	01 15	01 55	02 28	02 58
20	04 40	05 07	05 30	00 54	01 38	02 16	02 51
N 10	04 55	05 21	05 42	00 34	01 23	02 06	02 45
0	05 07	05 32	05 54	00 17	01 09	01 56	02 40
S 10	05 18	05 43	06 05	24 55	00 55	01 46	02 35
20	05 27	05 53	06 16	24 39	00 39	01 36	02 29
30	05 36	06 05	06 29	24 22	00 22	01 24	02 22
35	05 41	06 11	06 37	24 12	00 12	01 17	02 18
40	05 45	06 17	06 45	24 00	00 00	01 09	02 14
45	05 50	06 25	06 55	23 46	24 59	00 59	02 09
S 50	05 55	06 33	07 08	23 29	24 48	00 48	02 03
52	05 57	06 37	07 13	23 21	24 43	00 43	02 00
54	05 59	06 41	07 19	23 12	24 37	00 37	01 57
56	06 02	06 46	07 26	23 02	24 30	00 30	01 54
58	06 04	06 51	07 34	22 51	24 23	00 23	01 50
S 60	06 07	06 57	07 43	22 37	24 15	00 15	01 46

Sunset, Twilight and Moonset

Lat.	Sunset	Twilight Civil	Naut.	Moonset 1	2	3	4
N 72	22 15	////	////	■	08 36	11 46	14 00
N 70	21 32	////	////	■	09 38	12 05	14 07
68	21 03	23 07	////	■	10 12	12 20	14 12
66	20 42	22 08	////	08 15	10 37	12 33	14 17
64	20 25	21 36	////	08 54	10 56	12 43	14 21
62	20 11	21 12	23 13	09 22	11 11	12 51	14 24
60	19 59	20 54	22 20	09 42	11 24	12 59	14 27
N 58	19 49	20 38	21 50	10 00	11 35	13 05	14 30
56	19 41	20 26	21 28	10 14	11 45	13 11	14 32
54	19 33	20 15	21 11	10 26	11 53	13 16	14 34
52	19 26	20 05	20 56	10 37	12 01	13 20	14 36
50	19 20	19 57	20 44	10 47	12 07	13 24	14 38
45	19 06	19 39	20 19	11 07	12 22	13 33	14 42
N 40	18 55	19 25	20 01	11 23	12 33	13 41	14 45
35	18 46	19 13	19 46	11 37	12 43	13 47	14 47
30	18 38	19 03	19 33	11 48	12 52	13 52	14 50
20	18 24	18 47	19 14	12 09	13 07	14 02	14 54
N 10	18 12	18 34	18 59	12 26	13 20	14 10	14 57
0	18 00	18 22	18 47	12 42	13 32	14 17	15 00
S 10	17 49	18 11	18 36	12 58	13 44	14 25	15 03
20	17 38	18 00	18 27	13 15	13 56	14 33	15 07
30	17 24	17 49	18 17	13 34	14 11	14 42	15 10
35	17 17	17 43	18 13	13 46	14 19	14 47	15 13
40	17 08	17 36	18 08	13 59	14 28	14 53	15 15
45	16 58	17 29	18 04	14 14	14 39	15 00	15 18
S 50	16 46	17 20	17 58	14 32	14 52	15 08	15 21
52	16 40	17 16	17 56	14 41	14 58	15 12	15 23
54	16 34	17 12	17 54	14 50	15 05	15 16	15 24
56	16 27	17 07	17 51	15 01	15 12	15 20	15 26
58	16 19	17 02	17 49	15 14	15 21	15 25	15 28
S 60	16 11	16 56	17 46	15 28	15 31	15 31	15 30

Day	SUN Eqn. of Time 00ʰ	12ʰ	Mer. Pass.	MOON Mer. Pass. Upper	Lower	Age	Phase
1	02 51	02 54	11 57	06 29	18 56	22	
2	02 58	03 01	11 57	07 20	19 44	23	◐
3	03 05	03 08	11 57	08 07	20 29	24	

Table 2. Daily Page from The Nautical Almanac..

14ᵐ   INCREMENTS AND CORRECTIONS   15ᵐ

14ᵐ (s)	SUN PLANETS	ARIES	MOON	v or Corrⁿ d	v or Corrⁿ d	v or Corrⁿ d
00	3 30·0	3 30·6	3 20·4	0·0 0·0	6·0 1·5	12·0 2·9
01	3 30·3	3 30·8	3 20·7	0·1 0·0	6·1 1·5	12·1 2·9
02	3 30·5	3 31·1	3 20·9	0·2 0·0	6·2 1·5	12·2 2·9
03	3 30·8	3 31·3	3 21·1	0·3 0·1	6·3 1·5	12·3 3·0
04	3 31·0	3 31·6	3 21·4	0·4 0·1	6·4 1·5	12·4 3·0
05	3 31·3	3 31·8	3 21·6	0·5 0·1	6·5 1·6	12·5 3·0
06	3 31·5	3 32·1	3 21·9	0·6 0·1	6·6 1·6	12·6 3·0
07	3 31·8	3 32·3	3 22·1	0·7 0·2	6·7 1·6	12·7 3·1
08	3 32·0	3 32·6	3 22·3	0·8 0·2	6·8 1·6	12·8 3·1
09	3 32·3	3 32·8	3 22·6	0·9 0·2	6·9 1·7	12·9 3·1
10	3 32·5	3 33·1	3 22·8	1·0 0·2	7·0 1·7	13·0 3·1
11	3 32·8	3 33·3	3 23·1	1·1 0·3	7·1 1·7	13·1 3·2
12	3 33·0	3 33·6	3 23·3	1·2 0·3	7·2 1·7	13·2 3·2
13	3 33·3	3 33·8	3 23·5	1·3 0·3	7·3 1·8	13·3 3·2
14	3 33·5	3 34·1	3 23·8	1·4 0·3	7·4 1·8	13·4 3·2
15	3 33·8	3 34·3	3 24·0	1·5 0·4	7·5 1·8	13·5 3·3
16	3 34·0	3 34·6	3 24·3	1·6 0·4	7·6 1·8	13·6 3·3
17	3 34·3	3 34·8	3 24·5	1·7 0·4	7·7 1·9	13·7 3·3
18	3 34·5	3 35·1	3 24·7	1·8 0·4	7·8 1·9	13·8 3·3
19	3 34·8	3 35·3	3 25·0	1·9 0·5	7·9 1·9	13·9 3·4
20	3 35·0	3 35·6	3 25·2	2·0 0·5	8·0 1·9	14·0 3·4
21	3 35·3	3 35·8	3 25·4	2·1 0·5	8·1 2·0	14·1 3·4
22	3 35·5	3 36·1	3 25·7	2·2 0·5	8·2 2·0	14·2 3·4
23	3 35·8	3 36·3	3 25·9	2·3 0·6	8·3 2·0	14·3 3·5
24	3 36·0	3 36·6	3 26·2	2·4 0·6	8·4 2·0	14·4 3·5
25	3 36·3	3 36·8	3 26·4	2·5 0·6	8·5 2·1	14·5 3·5
26	3 36·5	3 37·1	3 26·6	2·6 0·6	8·6 2·1	14·6 3·5
27	3 36·8	3 37·3	3 26·9	2·7 0·7	8·7 2·1	14·7 3·6
28	3 37·0	3 37·6	3 27·1	2·8 0·7	8·8 2·1	14·8 3·6
29	3 37·3	3 37·8	3 27·4	2·9 0·7	8·9 2·2	14·9 3·6
30	3 37·5	3 38·1	3 27·6	3·0 0·7	9·0 2·2	15·0 3·6
31	3 37·8	3 38·3	3 27·8	3·1 0·7	9·1 2·2	15·1 3·6
32	3 38·0	3 38·6	3 28·1	3·2 0·8	9·2 2·2	15·2 3·7
33	3 38·3	3 38·8	3 28·3	3·3 0·8	9·3 2·2	15·3 3·7
34	3 38·5	3 39·1	3 28·5	3·4 0·8	9·4 2·3	15·4 3·7
35	3 38·8	3 39·3	3 28·8	3·5 0·8	9·5 2·3	15·5 3·7
36	3 39·0	3 39·6	3 29·0	3·6 0·9	9·6 2·3	15·6 3·8
37	3 39·3	3 39·9	3 29·3	3·7 0·9	9·7 2·3	15·7 3·8
38	3 39·5	3 40·1	3 29·5	3·8 0·9	9·8 2·4	15·8 3·8
39	3 39·8	3 40·4	3 29·7	3·9 0·9	9·9 2·4	15·9 3·8
40	3 40·0	3 40·6	3 30·0	4·0 1·0	10·0 2·4	16·0 3·9
41	3 40·3	3 40·9	3 30·2	4·1 1·0	10·1 2·4	16·1 3·9
42	3 40·5	3 41·1	3 30·5	4·2 1·0	10·2 2·5	16·2 3·9
43	3 40·8	3 41·4	3 30·7	4·3 1·0	10·3 2·5	16·3 3·9
44	3 41·0	3 41·6	3 30·9	4·4 1·1	10·4 2·5	16·4 4·0
45	3 41·3	3 41·9	3 31·2	4·5 1·1	10·5 2·5	16·5 4·0
46	3 41·5	3 42·1	3 31·4	4·6 1·1	10·6 2·6	16·6 4·0
47	3 41·8	3 42·4	3 31·6	4·7 1·1	10·7 2·6	16·7 4·0
48	3 42·0	3 42·6	3 31·9	4·8 1·2	10·8 2·6	16·8 4·1
49	3 42·3	3 42·9	3 32·1	4·9 1·2	10·9 2·6	16·9 4·1
50	3 42·5	3 43·1	3 32·4	5·0 1·2	11·0 2·7	17·0 4·1
51	3 42·8	3 43·4	3 32·6	5·1 1·2	11·1 2·7	17·1 4·1
52	3 43·0	3 43·6	3 32·8	5·2 1·3	11·2 2·7	17·2 4·2
53	3 43·3	3 43·9	3 33·1	5·3 1·3	11·3 2·7	17·3 4·2
54	3 43·5	3 44·1	3 33·3	5·4 1·3	11·4 2·8	17·4 4·2
55	3 43·8	3 44·4	3 33·6	5·5 1·3	11·5 2·8	17·5 4·2
56	3 44·0	3 44·6	3 33·8	5·6 1·4	11·6 2·8	17·6 4·3
57	3 44·3	3 44·9	3 34·0	5·7 1·4	11·7 2·8	17·7 4·3
58	3 44·5	3 45·1	3 34·3	5·8 1·4	11·8 2·9	17·8 4·3
59	3 44·8	3 45·4	3 34·5	5·9 1·4	11·9 2·9	17·9 4·3
60	3 45·0	3 45·6	3 34·8	6·0 1·5	12·0 2·9	18·0 4·4

15ᵐ (s)	SUN PLANETS	ARIES	MOON	v or Corrⁿ d	v or Corrⁿ d	v or Corrⁿ d
00	3 45·0	3 45·6	3 34·8	0·0 0·0	6·0 1·6	12·0 3·1
01	3 45·3	3 45·9	3 35·0	0·1 0·0	6·1 1·6	12·1 3·1
02	3 45·5	3 46·1	3 35·2	0·2 0·1	6·2 1·6	12·2 3·2
03	3 45·8	3 46·4	3 35·5	0·3 0·1	6·3 1·6	12·3 3·2
04	3 46·0	3 46·6	3 35·7	0·4 0·1	6·4 1·7	12·4 3·2
05	3 46·3	3 46·9	3 35·9	0·5 0·1	6·5 1·7	12·5 3·2
06	3 46·5	3 47·1	3 36·2	0·6 0·2	6·6 1·7	12·6 3·3
07	3 46·8	3 47·4	3 36·4	0·7 0·2	6·7 1·7	12·7 3·3
08	3 47·0	3 47·6	3 36·7	0·8 0·2	6·8 1·8	12·8 3·3
09	3 47·3	3 47·9	3 36·9	0·9 0·2	6·9 1·8	12·9 3·3
10	3 47·5	3 48·1	3 37·1	1·0 0·3	7·0 1·8	13·0 3·4
11	3 47·8	3 48·4	3 37·4	1·1 0·3	7·1 1·8	13·1 3·4
12	3 48·0	3 48·6	3 37·6	1·2 0·3	7·2 1·9	13·2 3·4
13	3 48·3	3 48·9	3 37·9	1·3 0·3	7·3 1·9	13·3 3·4
14	3 48·5	3 49·1	3 38·1	1·4 0·4	7·4 1·9	13·4 3·5
15	3 48·8	3 49·4	3 38·3	1·5 0·4	7·5 1·9	13·5 3·5
16	3 49·0	3 49·6	3 38·6	1·6 0·4	7·6 2·0	13·6 3·5
17	3 49·3	3 49·9	3 38·8	1·7 0·4	7·7 2·0	13·7 3·5
18	3 49·5	3 50·1	3 39·0	1·8 0·5	7·8 2·0	13·8 3·6
19	3 49·8	3 50·4	3 39·3	1·9 0·5	7·9 2·0	13·9 3·6
20	3 50·0	3 50·6	3 39·5	2·0 0·5	8·0 2·1	14·0 3·6
21	3 50·3	3 50·9	3 39·8	2·1 0·5	8·1 2·1	14·1 3·6
22	3 50·5	3 51·1	3 40·0	2·2 0·6	8·2 2·1	14·2 3·7
23	3 50·8	3 51·4	3 40·2	2·3 0·6	8·3 2·1	14·3 3·7
24	3 51·0	3 51·6	3 40·5	2·4 0·6	8·4 2·2	14·4 3·7
25	3 51·3	3 51·9	3 40·7	2·5 0·6	8·5 2·2	14·5 3·7
26	3 51·5	3 52·1	3 41·0	2·6 0·7	8·6 2·2	14·6 3·8
27	3 51·8	3 52·4	3 41·2	2·7 0·7	8·7 2·2	14·7 3·8
28	3 52·0	3 52·6	3 41·4	2·8 0·7	8·8 2·3	14·8 3·8
29	3 52·3	3 52·9	3 41·7	2·9 0·7	8·9 2·3	14·9 3·8
30	3 52·5	3 53·1	3 41·9	3·0 0·8	9·0 2·3	15·0 3·9
31	3 52·8	3 53·4	3 42·1	3·1 0·8	9·1 2·4	15·1 3·9
32	3 53·0	3 53·6	3 42·4	3·2 0·8	9·2 2·4	15·2 3·9
33	3 53·3	3 53·9	3 42·6	3·3 0·9	9·3 2·4	15·3 4·0
34	3 53·5	3 54·1	3 42·9	3·4 0·9	9·4 2·4	15·4 4·0
35	3 53·8	3 54·4	3 43·1	3·5 0·9	9·5 2·5	15·5 4·0
36	3 54·0	3 54·6	3 43·3	3·6 0·9	9·6 2·5	15·6 4·0
37	3 54·3	3 54·9	3 43·6	3·7 1·0	9·7 2·5	15·7 4·1
38	3 54·5	3 55·1	3 43·8	3·8 1·0	9·8 2·5	15·8 4·1
39	3 54·8	3 55·4	3 44·1	3·9 1·0	9·9 2·6	15·9 4·1
40	3 55·0	3 55·6	3 44·3	4·0 1·0	10·0 2·6	16·0 4·1
41	3 55·3	3 55·9	3 44·5	4·1 1·1	10·1 2·6	16·1 4·2
42	3 55·5	3 56·1	3 44·8	4·2 1·1	10·2 2·6	16·2 4·2
43	3 55·8	3 56·4	3 45·0	4·3 1·1	10·3 2·7	16·3 4·2
44	3 56·0	3 56·6	3 45·2	4·4 1·1	10·4 2·7	16·4 4·2
45	3 56·3	3 56·9	3 45·5	4·5 1·2	10·5 2·7	16·5 4·3
46	3 56·5	3 57·1	3 45·7	4·6 1·2	10·6 2·7	16·6 4·3
47	3 56·8	3 57·4	3 46·0	4·7 1·2	10·7 2·8	16·7 4·3
48	3 57·0	3 57·6	3 46·2	4·8 1·2	10·8 2·8	16·8 4·3
49	3 57·3	3 57·9	3 46·4	4·9 1·3	10·9 2·8	16·9 4·4
50	3 57·5	3 58·2	3 46·7	5·0 1·3	11·0 2·8	17·0 4·4
51	3 57·8	3 58·4	3 46·9	5·1 1·3	11·1 2·9	17·1 4·4
52	3 58·0	3 58·7	3 47·2	5·2 1·3	11·2 2·9	17·2 4·4
53	3 58·3	3 58·9	3 47·4	5·3 1·4	11·3 2·9	17·3 4·5
54	3 58·5	3 59·2	3 47·6	5·4 1·4	11·4 2·9	17·4 4·5
55	3 58·8	3 59·4	3 47·9	5·5 1·4	11·5 3·0	17·5 4·5
56	3 59·0	3 59·7	3 48·1	5·6 1·4	11·6 3·0	17·6 4·5
57	3 59·3	3 59·9	3 48·4	5·7 1·5	11·7 3·0	17·7 4·6
58	3 59·5	4 00·2	3 48·6	5·8 1·5	11·8 3·0	17·8 4·6
59	3 59·8	4 00·4	3 48·8	5·9 1·5	11·9 3·1	17·9 4·6
60	4 00·0	4 00·7	3 49·1	6·0 1·6	12·0 3·1	18·0 4·7

Table 3. An increment (yellow) page from The Nautical Almanac..

16ᵐ   INCREMENTS AND CORRECTIONS   17ᵐ

16ᵐ

16	SUN PLANETS	ARIES	MOON	v or Corrⁿ d	v or Corrⁿ d	v or Corrⁿ d
00	4 00·0	4 00·7	3 49·1	0·0 0·0	6·0 1·7	12·0 3·3
01	4 00·3	4 00·9	3 49·3	0·1 0·0	6·1 1·7	12·1 3·3
02	4 00·5	4 01·2	3 49·5	0·2 0·1	6·2 1·7	12·2 3·4
03	4 00·8	4 01·4	3 49·8	0·3 0·1	6·3 1·7	12·3 3·4
04	4 01·0	4 01·7	3 50·0	0·4 0·1	6·4 1·8	12·4 3·4
05	4 01·3	4 01·9	3 50·3	0·5 0·1	6·5 1·8	12·5 3·4
06	4 01·5	4 02·2	3 50·5	0·6 0·2	6·6 1·8	12·6 3·5
07	4 01·8	4 02·4	3 50·7	0·7 0·2	6·7 1·8	12·7 3·5
08	4 02·0	4 02·7	3 51·0	0·8 0·2	6·8 1·9	12·8 3·5
09	4 02·3	4 02·9	3 51·2	0·9 0·2	6·9 1·9	12·9 3·5
10	4 02·5	4 03·2	3 51·5	1·0 0·3	7·0 1·9	13·0 3·6
11	4 02·8	4 03·4	3 51·7	1·1 0·3	7·1 2·0	13·1 3·6
12	4 03·0	4 03·7	3 51·9	1·2 0·3	7·2 2·0	13·2 3·6
13	4 03·3	4 03·9	3 52·2	1·3 0·4	7·3 2·0	13·3 3·7
14	4 03·5	4 04·2	3 52·4	1·4 0·4	7·4 2·0	13·4 3·7
15	4 03·8	4 04·4	3 52·6	1·5 0·4	7·5 2·1	13·5 3·7
16	4 04·0	4 04·7	3 52·9	1·6 0·4	7·6 2·1	13·6 3·7
17	4 04·3	4 04·9	3 53·1	1·7 0·5	7·7 2·1	13·7 3·8
18	4 04·5	4 05·2	3 53·4	1·8 0·5	7·8 2·1	13·8 3·8
19	4 04·8	4 05·4	3 53·6	1·9 0·5	7·9 2·2	13·9 3·8
20	4 05·0	4 05·7	3 53·8	2·0 0·6	8·0 2·2	14·0 3·9
21	4 05·3	4 05·9	3 54·1	2·1 0·6	8·1 2·2	14·1 3·9
22	4 05·5	4 06·2	3 54·3	2·2 0·6	8·2 2·3	14·2 3·9
23	4 05·8	4 06·4	3 54·6	2·3 0·6	8·3 2·3	14·3 3·9
24	4 06·0	4 06·7	3 54·8	2·4 0·7	8·4 2·3	14·4 4·0
25	4 06·3	4 06·9	3 55·0	2·5 0·7	8·5 2·3	14·5 4·0
26	4 06·5	4 07·2	3 55·3	2·6 0·7	8·6 2·4	14·6 4·0
27	4 06·8	4 07·4	3 55·5	2·7 0·7	8·7 2·4	14·7 4·0
28	4 07·0	4 07·7	3 55·7	2·8 0·8	8·8 2·4	14·8 4·1
29	4 07·3	4 07·9	3 56·0	2·9 0·8	8·9 2·4	14·9 4·1
30	4 07·5	4 08·2	3 56·2	3·0 0·8	9·0 2·5	15·0 4·1
31	4 07·8	4 08·4	3 56·5	3·1 0·9	9·1 2·5	15·1 4·2
32	4 08·0	4 08·7	3 56·7	3·2 0·9	9·2 2·5	15·2 4·2
33	4 08·3	4 08·9	3 56·9	3·3 0·9	9·3 2·6	15·3 4·2
34	4 08·5	4 09·2	3 57·2	3·4 0·9	9·4 2·6	15·4 4·2
35	4 08·8	4 09·4	3 57·4	3·5 1·0	9·5 2·6	15·5 4·3
36	4 09·0	4 09·7	3 57·7	3·6 1·0	9·6 2·6	15·6 4·3
37	4 09·3	4 09·9	3 57·9	3·7 1·0	9·7 2·7	15·7 4·3
38	4 09·5	4 10·2	3 58·1	3·8 1·0	9·8 2·7	15·8 4·3
39	4 09·8	4 10·4	3 58·4	3·9 1·1	9·9 2·7	15·9 4·4
40	4 10·0	4 10·7	3 58·6	4·0 1·1	10·0 2·8	16·0 4·4
41	4 10·3	4 10·9	3 58·8	4·1 1·1	10·1 2·8	16·1 4·4
42	4 10·5	4 11·2	3 59·1	4·2 1·2	10·2 2·8	16·2 4·5
43	4 10·8	4 11·4	3 59·3	4·3 1·2	10·3 2·8	16·3 4·5
44	4 11·0	4 11·7	3 59·6	4·4 1·2	10·4 2·9	16·4 4·5
45	4 11·3	4 11·9	3 59·8	4·5 1·2	10·5 2·9	16·5 4·5
46	4 11·5	4 12·2	4 00·0	4·6 1·3	10·6 2·9	16·6 4·6
47	4 11·8	4 12·4	4 00·3	4·7 1·3	10·7 2·9	16·7 4·6
48	4 12·0	4 12·7	4 00·5	4·8 1·3	10·8 3·0	16·8 4·6
49	4 12·3	4 12·9	4 00·7	4·9 1·3	10·9 3·0	16·9 4·6
50	4 12·5	4 13·2	4 01·0	5·0 1·4	11·0 3·0	17·0 4·7
51	4 12·8	4 13·4	4 01·2	5·1 1·4	11·1 3·1	17·1 4·7
52	4 13·0	4 13·7	4 01·5	5·2 1·4	11·2 3·1	17·2 4·7
53	4 13·3	4 13·9	4 01·7	5·3 1·5	11·3 3·1	17·3 4·8
54	4 13·5	4 14·2	4 02·0	5·4 1·5	11·4 3·1	17·4 4·8
55	4 13·8	4 14·4	4 02·2	5·5 1·5	11·5 3·2	17·5 4·8
56	4 14·0	4 14·7	4 02·4	5·6 1·5	11·6 3·2	17·6 4·8
57	4 14·3	4 14·9	4 02·7	5·7 1·6	11·7 3·2	17·7 4·9
58	4 14·5	4 15·2	4 02·9	5·8 1·6	11·8 3·2	17·8 4·9
59	4 14·8	4 15·4	4 03·1	5·9 1·6	11·9 3·3	17·9 4·9
60	4 15·0	4 15·7	4 03·4	6·0 1·7	12·0 3·3	18·0 5·0

17ᵐ

17	SUN PLANETS	ARIES	MOON	v or Corrⁿ d	v or Corrⁿ d	v or Corrⁿ d
00	4 15·0	4 15·7	4 03·4	0·0 0·0	6·0 1·8	12·0 3·5
01	4 15·3	4 15·9	4 03·6	0·1 0·0	6·1 1·8	12·1 3·5
02	4 15·5	4 16·2	4 03·9	0·2 0·1	6·2 1·8	12·2 3·6
03	4 15·8	4 16·5	4 04·1	0·3 0·1	6·3 1·8	12·3 3·6
04	4 16·0	4 16·7	4 04·3	0·4 0·1	6·4 1·9	12·4 3·6
05	4 16·3	4 17·0	4 04·6	0·5 0·1	6·5 1·9	12·5 3·6
06	4 16·5	4 17·2	4 04·8	0·6 0·2	6·6 1·9	12·6 3·7
07	4 16·8	4 17·5	4 05·1	0·7 0·2	6·7 2·0	12·7 3·7
08	4 17·0	4 17·7	4 05·3	0·8 0·2	6·8 2·0	12·8 3·7
09	4 17·3	4 18·0	4 05·5	0·9 0·3	6·9 2·0	12·9 3·8
10	4 17·5	4 18·2	4 05·8	1·0 0·3	7·0 2·0	13·0 3·8
11	4 17·8	4 18·5	4 06·0	1·1 0·3	7·1 2·1	13·1 3·8
12	4 18·0	4 18·7	4 06·2	1·2 0·4	7·2 2·1	13·2 3·9
13	4 18·3	4 19·0	4 06·5	1·3 0·4	7·3 2·1	13·3 3·9
14	4 18·5	4 19·2	4 06·7	1·4 0·4	7·4 2·2	13·4 3·9
15	4 18·8	4 19·5	4 07·0	1·5 0·4	7·5 2·2	13·5 3·9
16	4 19·0	4 19·7	4 07·2	1·6 0·5	7·6 2·2	13·6 4·0
17	4 19·3	4 20·0	4 07·4	1·7 0·5	7·7 2·2	13·7 4·0
18	4 19·5	4 20·2	4 07·7	1·8 0·5	7·8 2·3	13·8 4·0
19	4 19·8	4 20·5	4 07·9	1·9 0·6	7·9 2·3	13·9 4·1
20	4 20·0	4 20·7	4 08·2	2·0 0·6	8·0 2·3	14·0 4·1
21	4 20·3	4 21·0	4 08·4	2·1 0·6	8·1 2·4	14·1 4·1
22	4 20·5	4 21·2	4 08·6	2·2 0·6	8·2 2·4	14·2 4·1
23	4 20·8	4 21·5	4 08·9	2·3 0·7	8·3 2·4	14·3 4·2
24	4 21·0	4 21·7	4 09·1	2·4 0·7	8·4 2·5	14·4 4·2
25	4 21·3	4 22·0	4 09·3	2·5 0·7	8·5 2·5	14·5 4·2
26	4 21·5	4 22·2	4 09·6	2·6 0·8	8·6 2·5	14·6 4·3
27	4 21·8	4 22·5	4 09·8	2·7 0·8	8·7 2·5	14·7 4·3
28	4 22·0	4 22·7	4 10·1	2·8 0·8	8·8 2·6	14·8 4·3
29	4 22·3	4 23·0	4 10·3	2·9 0·8	8·9 2·6	14·9 4·3
30	4 22·5	4 23·2	4 10·5	3·0 0·9	9·0 2·6	15·0 4·4
31	4 22·8	4 23·5	4 10·8	3·1 0·9	9·1 2·7	15·1 4·4
32	4 23·0	4 23·7	4 11·0	3·2 0·9	9·2 2·7	15·2 4·4
33	4 23·3	4 24·0	4 11·3	3·3 1·0	9·3 2·7	15·3 4·5
34	4 23·5	4 24·2	4 11·5	3·4 1·0	9·4 2·7	15·4 4·5
35	4 23·8	4 24·5	4 11·7	3·5 1·0	9·5 2·8	15·5 4·5
36	4 24·0	4 24·7	4 12·0	3·6 1·1	9·6 2·8	15·6 4·6
37	4 24·3	4 25·0	4 12·2	3·7 1·1	9·7 2·8	15·7 4·6
38	4 24·5	4 25·2	4 12·5	3·8 1·1	9·8 2·9	15·8 4·6
39	4 24·8	4 25·5	4 12·7	3·9 1·1	9·9 2·9	15·9 4·6
40	4 25·0	4 25·7	4 12·9	4·0 1·2	10·0 2·9	16·0 4·7
41	4 25·3	4 26·0	4 13·2	4·1 1·2	10·1 2·9	16·1 4·7
42	4 25·5	4 26·2	4 13·4	4·2 1·2	10·2 3·0	16·2 4·7
43	4 25·8	4 26·5	4 13·6	4·3 1·3	10·3 3·0	16·3 4·8
44	4 26·0	4 26·7	4 13·9	4·4 1·3	10·4 3·0	16·4 4·8
45	4 26·3	4 27·0	4 14·1	4·5 1·3	10·5 3·1	16·5 4·8
46	4 26·5	4 27·2	4 14·4	4·6 1·3	10·6 3·1	16·6 4·9
47	4 26·8	4 27·5	4 14·6	4·7 1·4	10·7 3·1	16·7 4·9
48	4 27·0	4 27·7	4 14·8	4·8 1·4	10·8 3·2	16·8 4·9
49	4 27·3	4 28·0	4 15·1	4·9 1·4	10·9 3·2	16·9 4·9
50	4 27·5	4 28·2	4 15·3	5·0 1·5	11·0 3·2	17·0 5·0
51	4 27·8	4 28·5	4 15·6	5·1 1·5	11·1 3·2	17·1 5·0
52	4 28·0	4 28·7	4 15·8	5·2 1·5	11·2 3·3	17·2 5·0
53	4 28·3	4 29·0	4 16·0	5·3 1·5	11·3 3·3	17·3 5·0
54	4 28·5	4 29·2	4 16·3	5·4 1·6	11·4 3·3	17·4 5·1
55	4 28·8	4 29·5	4 16·5	5·5 1·6	11·5 3·4	17·5 5·1
56	4 29·0	4 29·7	4 16·7	5·6 1·6	11·6 3·4	17·6 5·1
57	4 29·3	4 30·0	4 17·0	5·7 1·7	11·7 3·4	17·7 5·2
58	4 29·5	4 30·2	4 17·2	5·8 1·7	11·8 3·4	17·8 5·2
59	4 29·8	4 30·5	4 17·5	5·9 1·7	11·9 3·5	17·9 5·2
60	4 30·0	4 30·7	4 17·7	6·0 1·8	12·0 3·5	18·0 5·3

x

Table 4. An increment (yellow) page from The Nautical Almanac..

52ᵐ INCREMENTS AND CORRECTIONS 55ᵐ

52	SUN PLANETS	ARIES	MOON	v or Corrn d	v or Corrn d	v or Corrn d
s	° ′	° ′	° ′	′ ′	′ ′	′ ′
00	13 00·0	13 02·1	12 24·5	0·0 0·0	6·0 5·3	12·0 10·5
01	13 00·3	13 02·4	12 24·7	0·1 0·1	6·1 5·3	12·1 10·6
02	13 00·5	13 02·6	12 24·9	0·2 0·2	6·2 5·4	12·2 10·7
03	13 00·8	13 02·9	12 25·2	0·3 0·3	6·3 5·5	12·3 10·8
04	13 01·0	13 03·1	12 25·4	0·4 0·4	6·4 5·6	12·4 10·9
05	13 01·3	13 03·4	12 25·7	0·5 0·4	6·5 5·7	12·5 10·9
06	13 01·5	13 03·6	12 25·9	0·6 0·5	6·6 5·8	12·6 11·0
07	13 01·8	13 03·9	12 26·1	0·7 0·6	6·7 5·9	12·7 11·1
08	13 02·0	13 04·1	12 26·4	0·8 0·7	6·8 6·0	12·8 11·2
09	13 02·3	13 04·4	12 26·6	0·9 0·8	6·9 6·0	12·9 11·3
10	13 02·5	13 04·6	12 26·9	1·0 0·9	7·0 6·1	13·0 11·4
11	13 02·8	13 04·9	12 27·1	1·1 1·0	7·1 6·2	13·1 11·5
12	13 03·0	13 05·1	12 27·3	1·2 1·1	7·2 6·3	13·2 11·6
13	13 03·3	13 05·4	12 27·6	1·3 1·1	7·3 6·4	13·3 11·6
14	13 03·5	13 05·6	12 27·8	1·4 1·2	7·4 6·5	13·4 11·7
15	13 03·8	13 05·9	12 28·0	1·5 1·3	7·5 6·6	13·5 11·8
16	13 04·0	13 06·1	12 28·3	1·6 1·4	7·6 6·7	13·6 11·9
17	13 04·3	13 06·4	12 28·5	1·7 1·5	7·7 6·7	13·7 12·0
18	13 04·5	13 06·6	12 28·8	1·8 1·6	7·8 6·8	13·8 12·1
19	13 04·8	13 06·9	12 29·0	1·9 1·7	7·9 6·9	13·9 12·2
20	13 05·0	13 07·1	12 29·2	2·0 1·8	8·0 7·0	14·0 12·3
21	13 05·3	13 07·4	12 29·5	2·1 1·8	8·1 7·1	14·1 12·3
22	13 05·5	13 07·7	12 29·7	2·2 1·9	8·2 7·2	14·2 12·4
23	13 05·8	13 07·9	12 30·0	2·3 2·0	8·3 7·3	14·3 12·5
24	13 06·0	13 08·2	12 30·2	2·4 2·1	8·4 7·4	14·4 12·6
25	13 06·3	13 08·4	12 30·4	2·5 2·2	8·5 7·4	14·5 12·7
26	13 06·5	13 08·7	12 30·7	2·6 2·3	8·6 7·5	14·6 12·8
27	13 06·8	13 08·9	12 30·9	2·7 2·4	8·7 7·6	14·7 12·9
28	13 07·0	13 09·2	12 31·1	2·8 2·5	8·8 7·7	14·8 13·0
29	13 07·3	13 09·4	12 31·4	2·9 2·5	8·9 7·8	14·9 13·0
30	13 07·5	13 09·7	12 31·6	3·0 2·6	9·0 7·9	15·0 13·1
31	13 07·8	13 09·9	12 31·9	3·1 2·7	9·1 8·0	15·1 13·2
32	13 08·0	13 10·2	12 32·1	3·2 2·8	9·2 8·1	15·2 13·3
33	13 08·3	13 10·4	12 32·3	3·3 2·9	9·3 8·1	15·3 13·4
34	13 08·5	13 10·7	12 32·6	3·4 3·0	9·4 8·2	15·4 13·5
35	13 08·8	13 10·9	12 32·8	3·5 3·1	9·5 8·3	15·5 13·6
36	13 09·0	13 11·2	12 33·1	3·6 3·2	9·6 8·4	15·6 13·7
37	13 09·3	13 11·4	12 33·3	3·7 3·2	9·7 8·5	15·7 13·7
38	13 09·5	13 11·7	12 33·5	3·8 3·3	9·8 8·6	15·8 13·8
39	13 09·8	13 11·9	12 33·8	3·9 3·4	9·9 8·7	15·9 13·9
40	13 10·0	13 12·2	12 34·0	4·0 3·5	10·0 8·8	16·0 14·0
41	13 10·3	13 12·4	12 34·2	4·1 3·6	10·1 8·8	16·1 14·1
42	13 10·5	13 12·7	12 34·5	4·2 3·7	10·2 8·9	16·2 14·2
43	13 10·8	13 12·9	12 34·7	4·3 3·8	10·3 9·0	16·3 14·3
44	13 11·0	13 13·2	12 35·0	4·4 3·9	10·4 9·1	16·4 14·4
45	13 11·3	13 13·4	12 35·2	4·5 3·9	10·5 9·2	16·5 14·4
46	13 11·5	13 13·7	12 35·4	4·6 4·0	10·6 9·3	16·6 14·5
47	13 11·8	13 13·9	12 35·7	4·7 4·1	10·7 9·4	16·7 14·6
48	13 12·0	13 14·2	12 35·9	4·8 4·2	10·8 9·5	16·8 14·7
49	13 12·3	13 14·4	12 36·2	4·9 4·3	10·9 9·5	16·9 14·8
50	13 12·5	13 14·7	12 36·4	5·0 4·4	11·0 9·6	17·0 14·9
51	13 12·8	13 14·9	12 36·6	5·1 4·5	11·1 9·7	17·1 15·0
52	13 13·0	13 15·2	12 36·9	5·2 4·6	11·2 9·8	17·2 15·1
53	13 13·3	13 15·4	12 37·1	5·3 4·6	11·3 9·9	17·3 15·1
54	13 13·5	13 15·7	12 37·4	5·4 4·7	11·4 10·0	17·4 15·2
55	13 13·8	13 15·9	12 37·6	5·5 4·8	11·5 10·1	17·5 15·3
56	13 14·0	13 16·2	12 37·8	5·6 4·9	11·6 10·2	17·6 15·4
57	13 14·3	13 16·4	12 38·1	5·7 5·0	11·7 10·2	17·7 15·5
58	13 14·5	13 16·7	12 38·3	5·8 5·1	11·8 10·3	17·8 15·6
59	13 14·8	13 16·9	12 38·5	5·9 5·2	11·9 10·4	17·9 15·7
60	13 15·0	13 17·2	12 38·8	6·0 5·3	12·0 10·5	18·0 15·8

55	SUN PLANETS	ARIES	MOON	v or Corrn d	v or Corrn d	v or Corrn d
s	° ′	° ′	° ′	′ ′	′ ′	′ ′
00	13 45·0	13 47·3	13 07·4	0·0 0·0	6·0 5·6	12·0 11·1
01	13 45·3	13 47·5	13 07·7	0·1 0·1	6·1 5·6	12·1 11·2
02	13 45·5	13 47·8	13 07·9	0·2 0·2	6·2 5·7	12·2 11·3
03	13 45·8	13 48·0	13 08·1	0·3 0·3	6·3 5·8	12·3 11·4
04	13 46·0	13 48·3	13 08·4	0·4 0·4	6·4 5·9	12·4 11·5
05	13 46·3	13 48·5	13 08·6	0·5 0·5	6·5 6·0	12·5 11·6
06	13 46·5	13 48·8	13 08·8	0·6 0·6	6·6 6·1	12·6 11·7
07	13 46·8	13 49·0	13 09·1	0·7 0·6	6·7 6·2	12·7 11·7
08	13 47·0	13 49·3	13 09·3	0·8 0·7	6·8 6·3	12·8 11·8
09	13 47·3	13 49·5	13 09·6	0·9 0·8	6·9 6·4	12·9 11·9
10	13 47·5	13 49·8	13 09·8	1·0 0·9	7·0 6·5	13·0 12·0
11	13 47·8	13 50·0	13 10·0	1·1 1·0	7·1 6·6	13·1 12·1
12	13 48·0	13 50·3	13 10·3	1·2 1·1	7·2 6·7	13·2 12·2
13	13 48·3	13 50·5	13 10·5	1·3 1·2	7·3 6·8	13·3 12·3
14	13 48·5	13 50·8	13 10·8	1·4 1·3	7·4 6·8	13·4 12·4
15	13 48·8	13 51·0	13 11·0	1·5 1·4	7·5 6·9	13·5 12·5
16	13 49·0	13 51·3	13 11·2	1·6 1·5	7·6 7·0	13·6 12·6
17	13 49·3	13 51·5	13 11·5	1·7 1·6	7·7 7·1	13·7 12·7
18	13 49·5	13 51·8	13 11·7	1·8 1·7	7·8 7·2	13·8 12·8
19	13 49·8	13 52·0	13 12·0	1·9 1·8	7·9 7·3	13·9 12·9
20	13 50·0	13 52·3	13 12·2	2·0 1·9	8·0 7·4	14·0 13·0
21	13 50·3	13 52·5	13 12·4	2·1 1·9	8·1 7·5	14·1 13·0
22	13 50·5	13 52·8	13 12·7	2·2 2·0	8·2 7·6	14·2 13·1
23	13 50·8	13 53·0	13 12·9	2·3 2·1	8·3 7·7	14·3 13·2
24	13 51·0	13 53·3	13 13·1	2·4 2·2	8·4 7·8	14·4 13·3
25	13 51·3	13 53·5	13 13·4	2·5 2·3	8·5 7·9	14·5 13·4
26	13 51·5	13 53·8	13 13·6	2·6 2·4	8·6 8·0	14·6 13·5
27	13 51·8	13 54·0	13 13·9	2·7 2·5	8·7 8·0	14·7 13·6
28	13 52·0	13 54·3	13 14·1	2·8 2·6	8·8 8·1	14·8 13·7
29	13 52·3	13 54·5	13 14·3	2·9 2·7	8·9 8·2	14·9 13·8
30	13 52·5	13 54·8	13 14·6	3·0 2·8	9·0 8·3	15·0 13·9
31	13 52·8	13 55·0	13 14·8	3·1 2·9	9·1 8·4	15·1 14·0
32	13 53·0	13 55·3	13 15·1	3·2 3·0	9·2 8·5	15·2 14·1
33	13 53·3	13 55·5	13 15·3	3·3 3·1	9·3 8·6	15·3 14·2
34	13 53·5	13 55·8	13 15·5	3·4 3·1	9·4 8·7	15·4 14·2
35	13 53·8	13 56·0	13 15·8	3·5 3·2	9·5 8·8	15·5 14·3
36	13 54·0	13 56·3	13 16·0	3·6 3·3	9·6 8·9	15·6 14·4
37	13 54·3	13 56·5	13 16·2	3·7 3·4	9·7 9·0	15·7 14·5
38	13 54·5	13 56·8	13 16·5	3·8 3·5	9·8 9·1	15·8 14·6
39	13 54·8	13 57·0	13 16·7	3·9 3·6	9·9 9·2	15·9 14·7
40	13 55·0	13 57·3	13 17·0	4·0 3·7	10·0 9·3	16·0 14·8
41	13 55·3	13 57·5	13 17·2	4·1 3·8	10·1 9·3	16·1 14·9
42	13 55·5	13 57·8	13 17·4	4·2 3·9	10·2 9·4	16·2 15·0
43	13 55·8	13 58·0	13 17·7	4·3 4·0	10·3 9·5	16·3 15·1
44	13 56·0	13 58·3	13 17·9	4·4 4·1	10·4 9·6	16·4 15·2
45	13 56·3	13 58·5	13 18·2	4·5 4·2	10·5 9·7	16·5 15·3
46	13 56·5	13 58·8	13 18·4	4·6 4·3	10·6 9·8	16·6 15·4
47	13 56·8	13 59·0	13 18·6	4·7 4·3	10·7 9·9	16·7 15·4
48	13 57·0	13 59·3	13 18·9	4·8 4·4	10·8 10·0	16·8 15·5
49	13 57·3	13 59·5	13 19·1	4·9 4·5	10·9 10·1	16·9 15·6
50	13 57·5	13 59·8	13 19·3	5·0 4·6	11·0 10·2	17·0 15·7
51	13 57·8	14 00·0	13 19·6	5·1 4·7	11·1 10·3	17·1 15·8
52	13 58·0	14 00·3	13 19·8	5·2 4·8	11·2 10·4	17·2 15·9
53	13 58·3	14 00·5	13 20·1	5·3 4·9	11·3 10·5	17·3 16·0
54	13 58·5	14 00·8	13 20·3	5·4 5·0	11·4 10·5	17·4 16·1
55	13 58·8	14 01·0	13 20·5	5·5 5·1	11·5 10·6	17·5 16·2
56	13 59·0	14 01·3	13 20·8	5·6 5·2	11·6 10·7	17·6 16·3
57	13 59·3	14 01·5	13 21·0	5·7 5·3	11·7 10·8	17·7 16·4
58	13 59·5	14 01·8	13 21·3	5·8 5·4	11·8 10·9	17·8 16·5
59	13 59·8	14 02·0	13 21·5	5·9 5·5	11·9 11·0	17·9 16·6
60	14 00·0	14 02·3	13 21·7	6·0 5·6	12·0 11·1	18·0 16·7

Table 5. Increments and corrections from The Nautical Almanac..

A2 ALTITUDE CORRECTION TABLES 10°-90°—SUN, STARS, PLANETS

OCT.—MAR. **SUN** APR.—SEPT.						STARS AND PLANETS			DIP				
App. Alt.	Lower Limb	Upper Limb	App. Alt.	Lower Limb	Upper Limb	App. Alt.	Corr^n	App. Alt.	Additional Corr^n	Ht. of Eye	Corr^n	Ht. of Eye	Ht. of Eye Corr^n

OCT.—MAR. SUN		APR.—SEPT. SUN		STARS AND PLANETS Corr	STARS Additional	DIP (m)	DIP (ft)	DIP (m)
9 34 +10·8 −21·5		9 39 +10·6 −21·2		9 56	**1986**	m 2·4 −2·8	8·0	m 1·0 — 1·8
9 45 +10·9 −21·4		9 51 +10·7 −21·1		10 08 −5·3	**VENUS**	2·6 −2·9	8·6	1·5 — 2·2
9 56 +11·0 −21·3		10 03 +10·8 −21·0		10 20 −5·2	Jan. 1-July 20	2·8 −3·0	9·2	2·0 — 2·5
10 08 +11·1 −21·2		10 15 +10·9 −20·9		10 33 −5·1	° 60 + 0′·1	3·0 −3·1	9·8	2·5 — 2·8
10 21 +11·2 −21·1		10 27 +11·0 −20·8		10 46 −5·0		3·2 −3·2	10·5	3·0 — 3·0
10 34 +11·3 −21·0		10 40 +11·1 −20·7		11 00 −4·9	July 21-Sept. 8	3·4 −3·3	11·2	See table ←
10 47 +11·4 −20·9		10 54 +11·2 −20·6		11 14 −4·8	°	3·6 −3·4	11·9	
11 01 +11·5 −20·8		11 08 +11·3 −20·5		11 29 −4·7	41 + 0·2	3·8 −3·5	12·6	m
11 15 +11·6 −20·7		11 23 +11·4 −20·4		11 45 −4·6	76 + 0·1	4·0 −3·6	13·3	20 — 7·9
11 30 +11·7 −20·6		11 38 +11·5 −20·3		12 01 −4·5		4·3 −3·7	14·1	22 — 8·3
11 46 +11·8 −20·5		11 54 +11·6 −20·2		12 18 −4·4	Sept. 9-Oct. 1	4·5 −3·8	14·9	24 — 8·6
12 02 +11·9 −20·4		12 10 +11·7 −20·1		12 35 −4·3	Dec. 13-Dec. 31	4·7 −3·9	15·7	26 — 9·0
12 19 +12·0 −20·3		12 28 +11·8 −20·0		12 54 −4·2	°	5·0 −4·0	16·5	28 — 9·3
12 37 +12·1 −20·2		12 46 +11·9 −19·9		13 13 −4·1	34 + 0·3	5·2 −4·1	17·4	
12 55 +12·2 −20·1		13 05 +12·0 −19·8		13 33 −4·0	60 + 0·2	5·5 −4·2	18·3	30 — 9·6
13 14 +12·3 −20·0		13 24 +12·1 −19·7		13 54 −3·9	80 + 0·1	5·8 −4·3	19·1	32 —10·0
13 35 +12·4 −19·9		13 45 +12·2 −19·6		14 16 −3·8		6·1 −4·4	20·1	34 —10·3
13 56 +12·5 −19·8		14 07 +12·3 −19·5		14 40 −3·7	Oct. 2-Oct. 16	6·3 −4·5	21·0	36 —10·6
14 18 +12·6 −19·7		14 30 +12·4 −19·4		15 04 −3·6	Nov. 27-Dec. 12	6·6 −4·6	22·0	38 —10·8
14 42 +12·7 −19·6		14 54 +12·5 −19·3		15 30 −3·5	°	6·9 −4·7	22·9	
15 06 +12·8 −19·5		15 19 +12·6 −19·2		15 57 −3·4	29 + 0·4	7·2 −4·8	23·9	40 —11·1
15 32 +12·9 −19·4		15 46 +12·7 −19·1		16 26 −3·3	51 + 0·3	7·5 −4·9	24·9	42 —11·4
15 59 +13·0 −19·3		16 14 +12·8 −19·0		16 56 −3·2	68 + 0·2	7·9 −5·0	26·0	44 —11·7
16 28 +13·1 −19·2		16 44 +12·9 −18·9		17 28 −3·1	83 + 0·1	8·2 −5·1	27·1	46 —11·9
16 59 +13·2 −19·1		17 15 +13·0 −18·8		18 02 −3·0		8·5 −5·2	28·1	48 —12·2
17 32 +13·3 −19·0		17 48 +13·1 −18·7		18 38 −2·9	Oct. 17-Nov. 26	8·8 −5·3	29·2	
18 06 +13·4 −18·9		18 24 +13·2 −18·6		19 17 −2·8	°	9·2 −5·4	30·4	ft.
18 42 +13·5 −18·8		19 01 +13·3 −18·5		19 58 −2·7	26 + 0·5	9·5 −5·5	31·5	2 — 1·4
19 21 +13·6 −18·7		19 42 +13·4 −18·4		20 42 −2·6	46 + 0·4	9·9 −5·6	32·7	4 — 1·9
20 03 +13·7 −18·6		20 25 +13·5 −18·3		21 28 −2·5	60 + 0·3	10·3 −5·7	33·9	6 — 2·4
20 48 +13·8 −18·5		21 11 +13·6 −18·2		22 19 −2·4	73 + 0·2	10·6 −5·8	35·1	8 — 2·7
21 35 +13·9 −18·4		22 00 +13·7 −18·1		23 13 −2·3	84 + 0·1	11·0 −5·9	36·3	10 — 3·1
22 26 +14·0 −18·3		22 54 +13·8 −18·0		24 11 −2·2		11·4 −6·0	37·6	See table ←
23 22 +14·1 −18·2		23 51 +13·9 −17·9		25 14 −2·1	**MARS**	11·8 −6·1	38·9	
24 21 +14·2 −18·1		24 53 +14·0 −17·8		26 22 −2·0	Jan. 1-Apr. 6	12·2 −6·2	40·1	ft.
25 26 +14·3 −18·0		26 00 +14·1 −17·7		27 36 −1·9	Nov. 15-Dec. 31	12·6 −6·3	41·5	70 — 8·1
26 36 +14·4 −17·9		27 13 +14·2 −17·6		28 56 −1·8	°	13·0 −6·4	42·8	75 — 8·4
27 52 +14·5 −17·8		28 33 +14·3 −17·5		30 24 −1·7	60 + 0·1	13·4 −6·5	44·2	80 — 8·7
29 15 +14·6 −17·7		30 00 +14·4 −17·4		32 00 −1·6		13·8 −6·6	45·5	85 — 8·9
30 46 +14·7 −17·6		31 35 +14·5 −17·3		33 45 −1·5	Apr. 7-May 25	14·2 −6·7	46·9	90 — 9·2
32 26 +14·8 −17·5		33 20 +14·6 −17·2		35 40 −1·4	Sept. 13-Nov. 14	14·7 −6·8	48·4	95 — 9·5
34 17 +14·9 −17·4		35 17 +14·7 −17·1		37 48 −1·3	°	15·1 −6·9	49·8	
36 20 +15·0 −17·3		37 26 +14·8 −17·0		40 08 −1·2	41 + 0·2	15·5 −7·0	51·3	100 — 9·7
38 36 +15·1 −17·2		39 50 +14·9 −16·9		42 44 −1·1	76 + 0·1	16·0 −7·1	52·8	105 — 9·9
41 08 +15·2 −17·1		42 31 +15·0 −16·8		45 36 −1·0		16·5 −7·2	54·3	110 —10·2
43 59 +15·3 −17·0		45 31 +15·1 −16·7		48 47 −0·9	May 26-July 1	16·9 −7·3	55·8	115 —10·4
47 10 +15·4 −16·9		48 55 +15·2 −16·6		52 18 −0·8	Aug. 1-Sept. 12	17·4 −7·4	57·4	120 —10·6
50 46 +15·5 −16·8		52 44 +15·3 −16·5		56 11 −0·7	°	17·9 −7·5	58·9	125 —10·8
54 49 +15·6 −16·7		57 02 +15·4 −16·4		60 28 −0·6	34 + 0·3	18·4 −7·6	60·5	
59 23 +15·7 −16·6		61 51 +15·5 −16·3		65 08 −0·5	60 + 0·2	18·8 −7·7	62·1	130 —11·1
64 30 +15·8 −16·5		67 17 +15·6 −16·2		70 11 −0·4	80 + 0·1	19·3 −7·8	63·8	135 —11·3
70 12 +15·9 −16·4		73 16 +15·7 −16·1		75 34 −0·3		19·8 −7·9	65·4	140 —11·5
76 26 +16·0 −16·3		79 43 +15·8 −16·0		81 13 −0·2	July 2-July 31	20·4 −8·0	67·1	145 —11·7
83 05 +16·1 −16·2		86 32 +15·9 −15·9		87 03 −0·1	°	20·9 −8·1	68·8	150 —11·9
90 00		90 00		90 00 0·0	29 + 0·4	21·4	70·5	155 —12·1
					51 + 0·3			
					68 + 0·2			
					83 + 0·1			

App. Alt. = Apparent altitude = Sextant altitude corrected for index error and dip.

Table 6. 'Bookmark' from The Nautical Almanac..

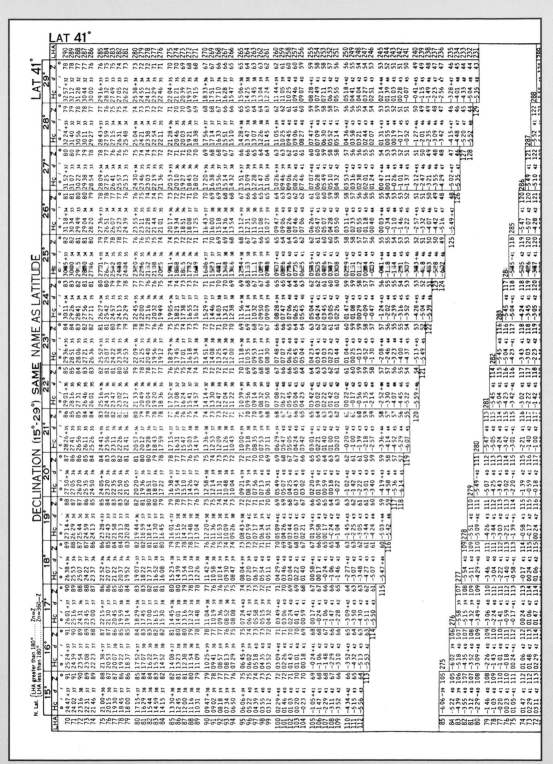

Table 7. A page from AP3270 Sight Reduction Tables for Air Navigation Volume III.

N. Lat. {LHA greater than 180°....... Zn=Z; LHA less than 180°........... Zn=360−Z}

DECLINATION (15°-29°) SAME NAME AS LATITUDE

LAT 49°

LHA	15° Hc	d	Z	16° Hc	d	Z	17° Hc	d	Z	18° Hc	d	Z	19° Hc	d	Z
	° ′	′	°	° ′	′	°	° ′	′	°	° ′	′	°	° ′	′	°
0	56 00	+60	180	57 00	+60	180	58 00	+60	180	59 00	+60	180	60 00	+60	180
1	55 59	60	178	56 59	60	178	57 59	60	178	58 59	60	178	59 59	60	178
2	55 58	60	177	56 58	60	177	57 58	60	176	58 58	59	176	59 57	60	176
3	55 55	60	175	56 55	59	175	57 54	60	175	58 54	60	175	59 54	60	174
4	55 51	59	173	56 50	60	173	57 50	60	173	58 50	60	173	59 50	59	173
5	55 45	+60	171	56 45	+60	171	57 45	+59	171	58 44	+60	171	59 44	+59	171
6	55 39	59	170	56 38	60	170	57 38	59	169	58 37	60	169	59 37	59	169
7	55 31	60	168	56 31	59	168	57 30	59	168	58 29	60	167	59 29	59	167
8	55 22	60	166	56 22	59	166	57 21	59	166	58 20	59	165	59 19	59	165
9	55 13	59	165	56 12	59	164	57 11	58	164	58 09	59	164	59 08	59	163
10	55 02	+58	163	56 00	+59	163	56 59	+59	162	57 58	+58	162	58 56	+59	161
11	54 50	58	161	55 48	59	161	56 47	58	161	57 45	58	160	58 43	58	160
12	54 36	59	160	55 35	58	159	56 33	58	159	57 31	58	158	58 29	58	158
13	54 22	58	158	55 20	58	158	56 18	58	158	57 16	58	157	58 14	57	156
14	54 07	58	157	55 05	57	156	56 02	58	156	57 00	57	155	57 57	57	154
15	53 51	+57	155	54 48	+58	154	55 46	+57	154	56 43	+57	153	57 40	+56	153
16	53 34	57	153	54 31	57	153	55 28	57	152	56 25	56	152	57 21	57	151
17	53 16	56	152	54 12	57	151	55 09	56	151	56 05	57	150	57 02	56	150
18	52 57	56	150	53 53	56	150	54 49	56	149	55 45	56	149	56 41	56	148
19	52 37	56	149	53 33	56	148	54 29	55	148	55 24	56	147	56 20	55	146
20	52 16	+56	147	53 12	+55	147	54 07	+55	146	55 02	+55	145	55 57	+55	145
21	51 54	55	146	52 49	56	145	53 45	55	145	54 40	54	144	55 34	55	143
22	51 32	55	144	52 27	54	144	53 21	55	143	54 16	54	143	55 10	54	142
23	51 08	55	143	52 03	54	142	52 57	55	142	53 52	53	141	54 45	54	140
24	50 44	55	142	51 39	54	141	52 33	53	140	53 26	54	140	54 20	53	139
25	50 19	+54	140	51 13	+54	140	52 07	+53	139	53 00	+54	138	53 54	+52	137
26	49 54	54	139	50 48	53	138	51 41	53	138	52 34	53	137	53 27	52	136
27	49 28	53	138	50 21	53	137	51 14	52	136	52 06	53	135	52 59	52	135
28	49 01	53	136	49 54	52	136	50 46	52	135	51 38	52	134	52 30	52	133
29	48 33	53	135	49 26	52	134	50 18	52	134	51 10	51	133	52 01	52	132
30	48 05	+52	134	48 57	+52	133	49 49	+52	132	50 41	+51	131	51 32	+51	131
31	47 36	52	133	48 28	52	132	49 20	51	131	50 11	51	130	51 02	50	129
32	47 07	51	131	47 58	52	131	48 50	50	130	49 40	51	129	50 31	50	128
33	46 37	51	130	47 28	51	129	48 19	50	128	49 09	51	128	50 00	49	127
34	46 07	51	129	46 58	50	128	47 48	50	127	48 38	50	127	49 28	49	126
35	45 36	+50	128	46 26	+50	127	47 16	+50	126	48 06	+50	125	48 56	+48	124
36	45 04	51	127	45 55	49	126	46 44	50	125	47 34	49	124	48 23	48	123
37	44 33	49	125	45 22	50	125	46 12	49	124	47 01	49	123	47 50	48	122
38	44 00	50	124	44 50	49	123	45 39	49	123	46 28	48	122	47 16	48	121
39	43 27	50	123	44 17	49	122	45 06	48	122	45 54	48	121	46 42	48	120
40	42 54	+49	122	43 43	+49	121	44 32	+48	120	45 20	+48	120	46 08	+47	119
41	42 21	48	121	43 09	49	120	43 58	48	119	44 46	47	119	45 33	47	118
42	41 47	48	120	42 35	48	119	43 23	48	118	44 11	47	118	44 58	47	117
43	41 13	48	119	42 01	47	118	42 48	48	117	43 36	47	116	44 23	46	116
44	40 38	48	118	41 26	47	117	42 13	47	116	43 00	47	115	43 47	46	115
45	40 03	+47	117	40 50	+48	116	41 38	+47	115	42 25	+46	114	43 11	+46	114
46	39 28	47	116	40 15	47	115	41 02	47	114	41 49	46	113	42 35	46	113
47	38 52	47	115	39 39	47	114	40 26	46	113	41 12	46	112	41 58	46	112
48	38 16	47	114	39 03	47	113	39 50	46	112	40 36	46	111	41 22	45	111
49	37 40	47	113	38 27	46	112	39 13	46	111	39 59	46	111	40 45	45	110
50	37 04	+46	112	37 50	+46	111	38 36	+46	110	39 22	+45	110	40 07	+46	109
51	36 27	46	111	37 13	46	110	37 59	46	109	38 45	45	109	39 30	45	108
52	35 50	46	110	36 36	46	109	37 22	45	109	38 07	46	108	38 53	44	107
53	35 13	46	109	35 59	46	108	36 45	45	108	37 30	45	107	38 15	44	106
54	34 36	46	108	35 22	45	108	36 07	45	107	36 52	45	106	37 37	44	105
55	33 58	+46	107	34 44	+45	107	35 29	+45	106	36 14	+45	105	36 59	+44	104
56	33 21	45	107	34 06	45	106	34 51	45	105	35 36	44	104	36 20	45	103
57	32 43	45	106	33 28	45	105	34 13	45	104	34 58	44	103	35 42	44	102
58	32 05	45	105	32 50	45	104	33 35	44	103	34 19	45	102	35 04	43	102
59	31 27	45	104	32 12	45	103	32 57	44	102	33 41	44	102	34 25	44	101
60	30 49	+44	103	31 33	+45	102	32 18	+44	102	33 02	+44	101	33 46	+44	100
61	30 10	45	102	30 55	44	102	31 39	45	101	32 24	43	100	33 07	44	99
62	29 32	44	101	30 16	45	101	31 01	44	100	31 45	44	99	32 29	43	98
63	28 53	45	101	29 38	44	100	30 22	44	99	31 06	44	98	31 50	43	98
64	28 14	45	100	28 59	44	99	29 43	44	98	30 27	43	98	31 10	44	97
65	27 35	+45	99	28 20	+44	98	29 04	+44	97	29 48	+43	97	30 31	+44	96
66	26 57	44	98	27 41	44	97	28 25	44	97	29 09	43	96	29 52	43	95
67	26 18	44	97	27 02	44	97	27 46	43	96	28 29	44	95	29 13	43	94
68	25 38	45	97	26 23	44	96	27 07	43	95	27 50	44	94	28 34	43	94
69	24 59	44	96	25 43	44	95	26 27	44	94	27 11	43	94	27 54	43	93

LHA	20° Hc	d	Z	21° Hc	d	Z	22° Hc	d	Z	23° Hc	d	Z	24° Hc	d	Z
	° ′	′	°	° ′	′	°	° ′	′	°	° ′	′	°	° ′	′	°
0	61 00	+60	180	62 00	+60	180	63 00	+60	180	64 00	+60	180	65 00	+60	180
1	60 59	60	178	61 59	60	178	62 59	60	178	63 59	60	178	64 59	60	178
2	60 57	60	176	61 57	60	176	62 57	60	176	63 57	60	176	64 57	60	176
3	60 54	60	174	61 54	60	174	62 54	60	174	63 54	59	174	64 53	60	174
4	60 49	60	172	61 49	60	172	62 49	60	172	63 49	59	172	64 48	60	171
5	60 43	+60	170	61 43	+60	170	62 43	+59	170	63 42	+60	170	64 42	+59	169
6	60 36	60	169	61 36	59	168	62 35	59	168	63 34	60	168	64 34	59	167
7	60 28	59	167	61 27	59	166	62 26	59	166	63 25	59	166	64 24	59	165
8	60 18	59	165	61 17	59	164	62 16	59	164	63 15	58	164	64 13	59	163
9	60 07	59	163	61 06	58	162	62 04	59	162	63 03	58	162	64 01	58	161
10	59 55	+58	161	60 53	+58	161	61 51	+59	160	62 50	+58	160	63 48	+58	159
11	59 41	58	159	60 39	58	159	61 37	58	158	62 35	58	158	63 33	57	157
12	59 27	58	157	60 25	57	157	61 22	58	156	62 20	57	156	63 17	57	155
13	59 11	57	156	60 08	58	155	61 06	57	154	62 03	57	154	63 00	56	153
14	58 54	57	154	59 51	57	153	60 48	57	153	61 45	56	152	62 41	56	151
15	58 36	+57	152	59 33	+57	152	60 30	+56	151	61 26	+56	150	62 22	+55	149
16	58 18	56	151	59 14	56	150	60 10	56	149	61 06	55	148	62 01	55	148
17	57 58	56	149	58 54	55	148	59 49	55	147	60 44	55	146	61 39	55	146
18	57 37	55	147	58 32	55	146	59 27	55	146	60 22	55	145	61 17	54	144
19	57 15	55	146	58 10	55	145	59 05	54	144	59 59	54	143	60 53	54	142
20	56 52	+55	144	57 47	+54	143	58 41	+54	142	59 35	+54	142	60 29	+53	141
21	56 29	54	142	57 23	54	142	58 17	53	141	59 10	53	140	60 03	53	139
22	56 04	54	141	56 58	53	140	57 51	53	139	58 44	53	138	59 37	52	137
23	55 39	53	139	56 32	53	139	57 25	53	138	58 18	52	137	59 10	52	136
24	55 13	53	138	56 06	52	137	56 58	53	136	57 51	51	135	58 42	52	134
25	54 46	+53	137	55 39	+52	136	56 31	+52	135	57 23	+51	134	58 14	+51	133
26	54 19	52	135	55 11	52	134	56 03	51	133	56 54	51	132	57 45	50	131
27	53 51	51	134	54 42	52	133	55 34	50	132	56 24	51	131	57 15	50	130
28	53 22	51	132	54 13	51	131	55 04	50	131	55 54	50	130	56 44	50	129
29	52 53	50	131	53 43	51	130	54 34	50	129	55 24	49	128	56 13	49	127
30	52 23	+50	130	53 13	+50	129	54 03	+49	128	54 52	+50	127	55 42	+48	126
31	51 52	50	128	52 42	50	128	53 32	49	127	54 21	48	126	55 09	48	125
32	51 21	50	127	52 11	49	126	53 00	48	125	53 48	49	124	54 37	47	123
33	50 49	49	126	51 38	49	125	52 27	49	124	53 16	48	123	54 04	47	122
34	50 17	49	125	51 06	48	124	51 54	48	123	52 42	48	122	53 30	47	121
35	49 44	+49	124	50 33	+48	123	51 21	+48	122	52 09	+47	121	52 56	+47	120
36	49 11	49	122	50 00	47	121	50 47	48	120	51 35	47	119	52 22	46	118
37	48 38	48	121	49 26	47	120	50 13	47	119	51 00	47	118	51 47	46	117
38	48 04	48	120	48 52	47	119	49 39	46	118	50 25	47	117	51 12	45	116
39	47 30	47	119	48 17	47	118	49 04	46	117	49 50	46	116	50 36	45	115
40	46 55	+47	118	47 42	+47	117	48 29	+46	116	49 15	+45	115	50 00	+45	114
41	46 20	47	117	47 07	46	116	47 53	46	115	48 39	45	114	49 24	45	113
42	45 45	46	116	46 31	46	115	47 17	46	114	48 03	45	113	48 48	44	112
43	45 09	46	115	45 55	46	114	46 41	45	113	47 26	45	112	48 11	44	111
44	44 33	46	114	45 19	46	113	46 05	45	112	46 50	44	111	47 34	44	110
45	43 57	+46	113	44 43	+45	112	45 28	+45	111	46 13	+44	110	46 57	+44	109
46	43 21	45	112	44 06	45	111	44 51	45	110	45 36	44	109	46 20	43	108
47	42 44	45	111	43 29	45	110	44 14	44	109	44 58	44	108	45 42	44	107
48	42 07	45	110	42 52	45	109	43 37	44	108	44 21	43	107	45 04	44	106
49	41 30	45	109	42 15	44	108	42 59	44	107	43 43	43	106	44 26	43	105
50	40 53	+44	108	41 37	+44	107	42 21	+44	106	43 05	+43	105	43 48	+43	104
51	40 15	44	107	40 59	44	106	41 43	44	105	42 27	43	104	43 10	43	103
52	39 37	44	106	40 21	44	105	41 05	44	104	41 49	43	103	42 32	42	102
53	38 59	44	105	39 43	44	104	40 27	43	103	41 10	43	103	41 53	42	102
54	38 21	44	104	39 05	44	103	39 49	43	102	40 32	43	102	41 15	42	101
55	37 43	+44	103	38 27	+43	103	39 10	+43	102	39 53	+43	101	40 36	+42	100
56	37 05	43	103	37 48	44	102	38 32	43	101	39 15	42	100	39 57	42	99
57	36 26	44	102	37 10	43	101	37 53	43	100	38 36	42	99	39 18	42	98
58	35 47	44	101	36 31	43	100	37 14	43	99	37 57	42	98	38 39	42	97
59	35 09	43	100	35 52	43	99	36 35	43	98	37 18	42	97	38 00	42	96
60	34 30	+43	99	35 13	+43	98	35 56	+43	97	36 39	+42	97	37 21	+42	96
61	33 51	43	98	34 34	43	97	35 17	43	97	36 00	42	96	36 42	41	95
62	33 12	43	98	33 55	43	97	34 38	42	96	35 20	42	95	36 02	42	94
63	32 33	43	97	33 16	43	96	33 59	42	95	34 41	42	94	35 23	42	93
64	31 54	43	96	32 37	42	95	33 19	43	94	34 02	42	93	34 44	41	93
65	31 15	+43	95	31 58	+42	94	32 40	+43	93	33 23	+41	93	34 04	+42	92
66	30 35	43	94	31 18	43	93	32 01	42	92	32 43	42	92	33 25	42	91
67	29 56	43	94	30 39	43	93	31 22	42	92	32 04	42	91	32 46	41	90
68	29 17	43	93	30 00	42	92	30 42	42	91	31 24	42	90	32 06	42	89
69	28 37	43	92	29 20	43	91	30 03	42	90	30 45	42	90	31 27	42	89

LHA	25° Hc	d	Z	26° Hc	d	Z	27° Hc	d	Z	28° Hc	d	Z	29° Hc	d	Z	LHA
	° ′	′	°	° ′	′	°	° ′	′	°	° ′	′	°	° ′	′	°	
0	66 00	+60	180	67 00	+60	180	68 00	+60	180	69 00	+60	180	70 00	+60	180	360
1	65 59	60	178	66 59	60	178	67 59	60	178	68 59	60	178	69 59	60	177	359
2	65 57	60	176	66 57	60	175	67 57	60	175	68 57	60	175	69 57	59	175	358
3	65 53	60	173	66 53	60	173	67 53	59	173	68 52	60	173	69 52	60	172	357
4	65 48	59	171	66 47	60	171	67 47	60	171	68 47	59	170	69 46	60	170	356
5	65 41	+59	169	66 40	+60	169	67 40	+59	168	68 39	+59	168	69 38	+59	167	355
6	65 33	59	167	66 32	59	166	67 31	59	166	68 30	59	165	69 29	59	165	354
7	65 23	59	165	66 22	59	164	67 21	58	164	68 19	59	163	69 18	58	163	353
8	65 12	58	163	66 10	59	162	67 09	58	161	68 07	58	161	69 05	58	160	352
9	64 59	58	160	65 58	58	160	66 56	57	159	67 53	58	159	68 51	57	158	351
10	64 46	+57	158	65 43	+58	158	66 41	+57	157	67 38	+57	156	68 35	+57	155	350
11	64 30	58	156	65 28	57	156	66 25	57	155	67 22	56	154	68 18	57	153	349
12	64 14	57	154	65 11	56	154	66 07	56	152	67 04	56	152	68 00	55	151	348
13	63 56	57	152	64 53	56	152	65 49	56	151	66 45	55	150	67 40	55	149	347
14	63 37	56	150	64 33	55	149	65 29	55	149	66 24	55	148	67 19	54	147	346
15	63 17	+56	149	64 13	+55	148	65 08	+55	147	66 03	+54	146	66 57	+54	145	345
16	62 56	55	147	63 51	55	146	64 46	54	145	65 40	54	144	66 34	53	143	344
17	62 34	55	145	63 29	54	144	64 23	53	143	65 16	53	142	66 09	53	141	343
18	62 11	54	143	63 05	53	142	63 58	53	141	64 51	53	140	65 44	52	139	342
19	61 47	53	141	62 40	53	140	63 33	53	139	64 26	51	138	65 17	52	137	341
20	61 22	+53	140	62 15	+52	139	63 07	+52	138	63 59	+51	137	64 50	+51	135	340
21	60 56	52	138	61 48	52	137	62 40	51	136	63 31	51	135	64 22	50	134	339
22	60 29	52	136	61 21	51	135	62 12	51	134	63 03	50	133	63 53	50	132	338
23	60 02	51	135	60 53	51	134	61 44	50	133	62 34	49	132	63 23	49	130	337
24	59 34	50	133	60 24	50	132	61 14	50	130	62 04	49	129	62 53	48	129	336
25	59 05	+50	132	59 55	+49	131	60 44	+50	130	61 34	+48	128	62 22	+48	127	335
26	58 35	50	130	59 25	49	129	60 14	48	128	61 02	48	127	61 50	48	126	334
27	58 05	49	129	58 54	49	128	59 43	48	127	60 31	47	126	61 18	47	124	333
28	57 34	48	128	58 22	49	126	59 11	47	125	59 58	47	124	60 45	46	123	332
29	57 02	48	126	57 50	48	125	58 38	47	124	59 25	47	123	60 12	46	121	331
30	56 30	+48	125	57 18	+47	124	58 05	+47	123	58 52	+46	121	59 38	+45	120	330
31	55 57	48	124	56 45	47	122	57 32	46	121	58 18	46	120	59 04	45	119	329
32	55 24	48	122	56 12	46	121	56 58	46	120	57 44	45	119	58 29	45	118	328
33	54 51	47	121	55 38	46	120	56 24	45	119	57 09	45	118	57 54	44	116	327
34	54 17	46	120	55 03	46	119	55 49	45	118	56 34	45	116	57 19	43	115	326
35	53 43	+46	119	54 29	+45	118	55 14	+45	116	55 59	+44	115	56 43	+43	114	325
36	53 08	45	117	53 53	46	116	54 39	44	115	55 23	44	114	56 07	43	113	324
37	52 33	45	116	53 18	45	115	54 03	44	114	54 47	43	113	55 30	43	112	323
38	51 57	45	115	52 42	45	114	53 27	43	113	54 10	43	112	54 53	43	111	322
39	51 21	45	114	52 06	44	113	52 50	44	112	53 34	42	111	54 16	43	110	321
40	50 45	+45	113	51 30	+44	112	52 14	+43	111	52 57	+42	110	53 39	+42	109	320
41	50 09	44	112	50 53	44	111	51 37	43	110	52 20	42	109	53 02	41	107	319
42	49 32	44	111	50 16	43	110	50 59	43	109	51 42	42	108	52 24	41	106	318
43	48 55	44	110	49 39	43	109	50 22	43	108	51 05	41	107	51 46	41	105	317
44	48 18	44	109	49 02	42	108	49 44	43	107	50 27	41	106	51 08	41	105	316
45	47 41	+43	108	48 24	+43	107	49 07	+42	106	49 49	+41	105	50 30	+41	104	315
46	47 03	43	107	47 46	43	106	48 29	42	105	49 11	41	104	49 52	40	103	314
47	46 26	42	106	47 08	43	105	47 51	41	104	48 32	41	103	49 13	41	102	313
48	45 48	42	105	46 30	42	104	47 12	42	103	47 54	41	102	48 35	40	101	312
49	45 09	43	104	45 52	42	103	46 34	41	102	47 15	41	101	47 56	40	100	311
50	44 31	+43	103	45 14	+41	102	45 55	+41	101	46 36	+41	100	47 17	+40	99	310
51	43 53	42	102	44 35	42	101	45 17	41	100	45 58	40	99	46 38	40	98	309
52	43 14	42	101	43 56	42	100	44 38	41	99	45 19	40	98	45 59	40	97	308
53	42 36	42	101	43 18	41	100	43 59	41	99	44 40	40	98	45 20	40	97	307
54	41 57	42	100	42 39	41	99	43 20	41	98	44 01	40	97	44 41	40	96	306
55	41 18	+42	99	42 00	+41	98	42 41	+41	97	43 22	+40	96	44 02	+39	95	305
56	40 39	42	98	41 21	41	97	42 02	40	96	42 42	40	95	43 22	40	94	304
57	40 00	42	97	40 42	41	96	41 23	40	95	42 03	40	94	42 43	40	93	303
58	39 21	41	96	40 02	41	95	40 43	41	94	41 24	40	93	42 04	39	92	302
59	38 42	41	96	39 23	41	95	40 04	41	94	40 45	40	93	41 25	39	92	301
60	38 03	+41	95	38 44	+41	94	39 25	+40	93	40 05	+40	92	40 45	+40	91	300
61	37 23	42	94	38 05	41	93	38 46	40	92	39 26	40	91	40 06	39	90	299
62	36 44	41	93	37 25	41	92	38 06	41	91	38 47	39	90	39 26	40	89	298
63	36 05	41	92	36 46	41	92	37 27	40	91	38 07	40	90	38 47	40	89	297
64	35 25	42	92	36 07	40	91	36 47	41	90	37 28	40	89	38 08	39	88	296
65	34 46	+41	91	35 27	+41	90	36 08	+40	89	36 48	+40	88	37 28	+40	87	295
66	34 07	41	90	34 48	41	89	35 29	40	88	36 09	40	87	36 49	40	86	294
67	33 27	42	89	34 09	40	88	34 49	41	88	35 30	40	87	36 10	39	86	293
68	32 48	41	89	33 29	41	88	34 10	41	87	34 51	40	86	35 31	39	85	292
69	32 09	41	88	32 50	41	87	33 31	40	86	34 11	40	85	34 51	40	84	291

S. Lat. {LHA greater than 180°....... Zn=180−Z; LHA less than 180°........... Zn=180+Z}

DECLINATION (15°-29°) SAME NAME AS LATITUDE

Table 8. A page from AP3270 Sight Reduction Tables for Air Navigation Volume III.

TABLE 5.—Correction to Tabulated Altitude for Minutes of Declination

d /	1 2	3	4	5 6	7	8	9 10 11 12	13 14	15 16 17	18 19 20 21	22 23 24	25 26	27 28	29 30	31 32 33	34 35 36	37 38 39	40 41	42	43 44 45	46 47 48	49 50 51	52 53 54	55 56 57	58 59 60	d /

Table 9. Bookmark and inside back cover of AP3270 Volume II and III.

LAT 10°S

LHA ♈	Hc	Zn	Hc	Zn	Hc	Zn	Hc	Zn	Hc	Zn	Hc	Zn	Hc	Zn
	•Alpheratz		Hamal		ALDEBARAN		•RIGEL		ACHERNAR		•FOMALHAUT		Enif	
0	50 57	003	44 31	042	17 01	069	12 42	096	39 07	163	65 23	215	50 41	299
1	50 59	001	45 10	041	17 57	069	13 41	096	39 24	164	64 49	216	49 49	298
2	51 00	000	45 49	041	18 52	069	14 40	096	39 40	165	64 14	218	48 57	298
3	50 59	358	46 27	040	19 47	068	15 39	096	39 55	165	63 37	219	48 05	297
4	50 56	357	47 04	039	20 42	068	16 37	096	40 10	166	62 59	220	47 12	296
5	50 53	356	47 41	038	21 36	068	17 36	096	40 24	166	62 21	222	46 19	296
6	50 48	354	48 16	037	22 31	067	18 35	095	40 38	167	61 41	223	45 25	295
7	50 41	353	48 51	035	23 25	067	19 34	095	40 50	168	61 00	224	44 32	295
8	50 33	352	49 25	034	24 20	067	20 33	095	41 03	168	60 19	225	43 38	294
9	50 24	350	49 58	033	25 14	066	21 31	095	41 14	169	59 37	226	42 44	293
10	50 13	349	50 30	032	26 08	066	22 30	095	41 25	170	58 54	227	41 50	293
11	50 01	348	51 00	031	27 02	066	23 29	095	41 35	170	58 10	228	40 55	292
12	49 48	346	51 30	030	27 56	065	24 28	095	41 45	171	57 26	229	40 00	292
13	49 33	345	51 59	028	28 49	065	25 27	094	41 53	172	56 41	230	39 05	291
14	49 17	344	52 26	027	29 42	064	26 26	094	42 01	173	55 56	230	38 10	291
	Hamal		ALDEBARAN		•RIGEL		ACHERNAR		•FOMALHAUT		Enif		•Alpheratz	
15	52 53	026	30 36	064	27 25	094	42 09	173	55 10	231	37 15	291	49 00	342
16	53 18	024	31 29	064	28 24	094	42 15	174	54 24	232	36 20	290	48 41	341
17	53 41	023	32 21	063	29 23	094	42 21	175	53 37	232	35 24	290	48 22	340
18	54 04	022	33 14	063	30 22	094	42 26	175	52 50	233	34 28	289	48 01	339
19	54 25	020	34 06	062	31 21	094	42 31	176	52 03	234	33 33	289	47 39	338
20	54 44	019	34 58	062	32 20	093	42 34	177	51 15	234	32 37	289	47 16	336
21	55 02	017	35 50	061	33 19	093	42 37	178	50 27	235	31 41	288	46 51	335
22	55 19	016	36 42	061	34 18	093	42 39	178	49 38	235	30 44	288	46 26	334
23	55 34	014	37 33	060	35 17	093	42 41	179	48 50	236	29 48	287	46 00	333
24	55 48	012	38 24	060	36 16	093	42 41	180	48 01	236	28 52	287	45 33	332
25	56 00	011	39 15	059	37 15	093	42 41	181	47 12	237	27 55	287	45 04	331
26	56 10	009	40 06	058	38 14	093	42 40	181	46 22	237	26 59	286	44 35	330
27	56 19	008	40 56	058	39 13	092	42 38	182	45 32	237	26 02	286	44 05	329
28	56 25	006	41 46	057	40 12	092	42 36	183	44 43	238	25 05	286	43 34	328
29	56 31	004	42 35	056	41 11	092	42 33	183	43 52	238	24 08	286	43 02	327
	CAPELLA		•BETELGEUSE		SIRIUS		CANOPUS		•ACHERNAR		FOMALHAUT		•Alpheratz	
30	18 58	034	29 07	076	20 48	104	22 27	143	42 29	184	43 02	238	42 30	326
31	19 31	033	30 04	075	21 45	104	23 02	143	42 24	185	42 12	239	41 56	325
32	20 03	033	31 01	075	22 43	104	23 37	144	42 19	186	41 21	239	41 22	324
33	20 34	032	31 58	075	23 40	104	24 12	144	42 13	186	40 31	239	40 47	323
34	21 06	032	32 55	074	24 37	104	24 47	144	42 06	187	39 40	240	40 12	323
35	21 36	031	33 52	074	25 35	104	25 22	144	41 58	188	38 49	240	39 36	322
36	22 07	031	34 49	074	26 32	104	25 56	144	41 50	188	37 58	240	38 59	321
37	22 37	030	35 45	073	27 29	104	26 31	145	41 41	189	37 06	240	38 21	320
38	23 06	030	36 42	073	28 27	104	27 05	145	41 31	190	36 15	240	37 43	319
39	23 35	029	37 38	072	29 24	104	27 39	145	41 21	191	35 24	241	37 04	319
40	24 04	029	38 35	072	30 22	104	28 13	145	41 09	191	34 32	241	36 25	318
41	24 32	028	39 31	072	31 19	104	28 46	146	40 58	192	33 41	241	35 45	317
42	24 59	027	40 27	071	32 17	104	29 20	146	40 45	193	32 49	241	35 04	317
43	25 26	027	41 23	071	33 14	103	29 53	146	40 32	193	31 57	241	34 23	316
44	25 52	026	42 18	070	34 11	103	30 26	146	40 18	194	31 05	241	33 42	315
	CAPELLA		•BETELGEUSE		SIRIUS		CANOPUS		•ACHERNAR		FOMALHAUT		•Alpheratz	
45	26 18	026	43 14	070	35 09	103	30 58	147	40 04	194	30 14	241	33 00	315
46	26 44	025	44 09	069	36 06	103	31 30	147	39 49	195	29 22	241	32 18	314
47	27 08	024	45 04	069	37 04	103	32 02	147	39 33	196	28 30	242	31 35	313
48	27 32	024	45 59	068	38 01	103	32 34	148	39 17	196	27 38	242	30 52	313
49	27 56	023	46 54	068	38 59	103	33 05	148	39 00	197	26 46	242	30 08	312
50	28 19	022	47 49	067	39 56	103	33 36	148	38 42	197	25 54	242	29 24	312
51	28 41	022	48 43	066	40 54	103	34 07	149	38 24	198	25 02	242	28 40	311
52	29 02	021	49 37	066	41 51	104	34 38	149	38 06	199	24 10	242	27 55	311
53	29 23	020	50 31	065	42 49	104	35 08	150	37 47	199	23 18	242	27 10	310
54	29 44	020	51 24	064	43 46	104	35 37	150	37 27	200	22 26	242	26 25	310
55	30 03	019	52 18	064	44 44	104	36 06	151	37 07	200	21 33	242	25 39	309
56	30 22	018	53 10	063	45 41	104	36 35	151	36 46	201	20 41	242	24 53	309
57	30 40	018	54 03	062	46 38	104	37 04	152	36 25	201	19 49	242	24 07	308
58	30 58	017	54 55	061	47 36	104	37 32	152	36 03	202	18 57	242	23 20	308
59	31 14	016	55 47	061	48 33	104	37 59	152	35 41	202	18 05	242	22 34	307
	•CAPELLA		POLLUX		•SIRIUS		CANOPUS		ACHERNAR		•Diphda		Hamal	
60	31 30	015	23 46	053	49 30	104	38 26	153	35 19	203	41 39	255	46 33	321
61	31 45	015	24 33	053	50 28	104	38 53	154	34 56	203	40 42	255	45 55	320
62	32 00	014	25 20	052	51 25	104	39 19	154	34 32	204	39 45	255	45 17	319
63	32 14	013	26 07	052	52 22	104	39 44	155	34 08	204	38 48	255	44 37	318
64	32 26	012	26 53	051	53 19	105	40 09	155	33 44	205	37 51	255	43 57	317
65	32 39	011	27 39	051	54 17	105	40 34	156	33 19	205	36 54	255	43 16	316
66	32 50	011	28 24	050	55 14	105	40 58	156	32 54	205	35 57	255	42 35	315
67	33 00	010	29 10	050	56 11	105	41 21	157	32 29	206	34 59	255	41 53	314
68	33 10	009	29 55	049	57 08	105	41 44	158	32 03	206	34 02	255	41 11	314
69	33 19	008	30 39	049	58 05	106	42 06	158	31 37	206	33 05	255	40 28	313
70	33 27	007	31 24	048	59 02	106	42 28	159	31 10	207	32 08	255	39 44	312
71	33 34	007	32 07	048	59 58	106	42 49	160	30 43	207	31 11	255	39 00	311
72	33 40	006	32 51	047	60 55	106	43 09	160	30 16	208	30 14	255	38 15	311
73	33 46	005	33 34	046	61 52	107	43 28	161	29 48	208	29 17	255	37 30	310
74	33 51	004	34 16	046	62 48	107	43 47	162	29 21	208	28 20	255	36 45	309
	CAPELLA		POLLUX		•REGULUS		CANOPUS		•ACHERNAR		Diphda		•Hamal	
75	33 54	003	34 58	045	10 30	076	44 05	162	28 53	209	27 23	255	35 59	309
76	33 57	002	35 40	044	11 27	075	44 23	163	28 24	209	26 26	255	35 13	308
77	33 59	002	36 21	044	12 24	075	44 39	164	27 56	209	25 29	255	34 26	308
78	34 01	001	37 02	043	13 21	075	44 55	165	27 27	209	24 32	255	33 39	307
79	34 01	000	37 42	042	14 18	075	45 11	166	26 58	210	23 35	255	32 52	306
80	34 00	359	38 21	042	15 15	074	45 25	166	26 28	210	22 38	254	32 04	306
81	33 59	358	39 00	041	16 12	074	45 39	167	25 59	210	21 41	254	31 16	305
82	33 57	357	39 38	040	17 09	074	45 51	168	25 29	210	20 45	254	30 28	305
83	33 54	357	40 16	039	18 06	074	46 03	169	24 59	211	19 48	254	29 39	304
84	33 50	356	40 53	038	19 02	073	46 14	170	24 29	211	18 51	254	28 50	304
85	33 45	355	41 29	037	19 59	073	46 25	170	23 59	211	17 54	254	28 01	303
86	33 39	354	42 05	037	20 56	073	46 34	171	23 28	211	16 57	254	27 12	303
87	33 33	353	42 40	036	21 52	073	46 42	172	22 57	211	16 00	254	26 22	303
88	33 25	352	43 14	035	22 48	072	46 50	173	22 26	212	15 04	254	25 32	302
89	33 17	352	43 47	034	23 45	072	46 57	174	21 55	212	14 07	254	24 42	302

LAT 10°S

LHA ♈	Hc	Zn	Hc	Zn	Hc	Zn	Hc	Zn	Hc	Zn	Hc	Zn	Hc	Zn
	POLLUX		•REGULUS		Suhail		•CANOPUS		Acamar		•ALDEBARAN		CAPELLA	
90	44 19	033	24 41	072	37 30	138	47 03	175	39 37	225	56 12	321	33 08	351
91	44 51	032	25 37	071	38 09	138	47 08	176	38 55	225	55 34	320	32 58	350
92	45 22	031	26 33	071	38 48	139	47 12	177	38 13	226	54 56	319	32 48	349
93	45 52	030	27 29	071	39 27	139	47 15	177	37 31	226	54 17	318	32 36	348
94	46 21	029	28 24	070	40 05	140	47 17	178	36 48	226	53 36	316	32 24	348
95	46 48	028	29 20	070	40 43	140	47 18	179	36 05	227	52 55	315	32 11	347
96	47 15	027	30 15	070	41 21	141	47 19	180	35 22	227	52 13	314	31 57	346
97	47 41	025	31 11	069	41 58	141	47 18	181	34 39	227	51 31	313	31 42	345
98	48 06	024	32 06	069	42 35	142	47 17	182	33 55	228	50 47	312	31 27	345
99	48 30	023	33 01	068	43 11	142	47 14	183	33 11	228	50 03	311	31 11	344
100	48 52	022	33 56	068	43 47	143	47 11	184	32 27	228	49 18	310	30 54	343
101	49 14	021	34 50	068	44 23	143	47 07	185	31 43	228	48 33	309	30 36	342
102	49 34	019	35 45	067	44 58	144	47 02	185	30 59	229	47 47	309	30 18	342
103	49 53	018	36 39	067	45 32	145	46 56	186	30 15	229	47 01	308	29 59	341
104	50 11	017	37 34	066	46 06	145	46 49	187	29 30	229	46 14	307	29 39	340
	POLLUX		•REGULUS		Suhail		•CANOPUS		RIGEL		•ALDEBARAN		CAPELLA	
105	50 27	015	38 28	066	46 39	146	46 41	188	63 44	272	45 26	306	29 19	339
106	50 42	014	39 21	065	47 12	147	46 32	189	62 45	271	44 38	305	28 58	339
107	50 56	013	40 15	065	47 44	147	46 23	190	61 46	271	43 50	305	28 36	338
108	51 08	011	41 08	064	48 16	148	46 12	191	60 47	271	43 01	304	28 14	337
109	51 19	010	42 01	064	48 47	149	46 01	191	59 48	271	42 12	303	27 51	337
110	51 29	009	42 54	063	49 17	150	45 49	192	58 49	271	41 22	303	27 27	336
111	51 37	007	43 47	062	49 46	151	45 36	193	57 50	270	40 32	302	27 03	336
112	51 44	006	44 39	062	50 15	151	45 22	194	56 51	270	39 42	301	26 38	335
113	51 49	004	45 31	061	50 43	152	45 08	195	55 51	270	38 51	301	26 13	334
114	51 53	003	46 22	061	51 10	153	44 52	195	54 52	270	38 00	300	25 47	334
115	51 55	002	47 14	060	51 36	154	44 36	196	53 53	270	37 09	300	25 20	333
116	51 56	000	48 05	059	52 01	155	44 19	197	52 54	270	36 18	299	24 53	332
117	51 56	359	48 55	058	52 25	156	44 02	198	51 55	269	35 26	299	24 26	332
118	51 54	357	49 45	058	52 49	157	43 44	198	50 56	269	34 34	298	23 58	331
119	51 50	356	50 35	057	53 11	158	43 25	199	49 57	269	33 42	298	23 29	331
	•REGULUS		SPICA		•ACRUX		CANOPUS		RIGEL		•BETELGEUSE		POLLUX	
120	51 24	056	10 32	100	19 28	154	43 05	200	48 58	269	54 12	298	51 45	354
121	52 13	055	11 31	099	19 54	154	42 45	200	47 59	269	53 20	297	51 39	353
122	53 01	054	12 29	099	20 20	154	42 24	201	47 00	269	52 27	296	51 31	352
123	53 48	053	13 27	099	20 46	154	42 02	202	46 01	268	51 34	296	51 21	350
124	54 35	052	14 26	099	21 12	154	41 40	202	45 02	268	50 41	295	51 11	349
125	55 22	051	15 24	099	21 37	155	41 17	203	44 03	268	49 47	294	50 58	347
126	56 07	050	16 22	099	22 02	155	40 53	204	43 03	268	48 53	294	50 45	346
127	56 52	049	17 21	099	22 27	155	40 29	204	42 04	268	47 59	293	50 30	345
128	57 36	048	18 19	098	22 52	155	40 05	205	41 05	268	47 04	292	50 14	343
129	58 20	046	19 18	098	23 17	155	39 40	205	40 06	268	46 09	292	49 57	342
130	59 02	045	20 16	098	23 41	156	39 14	206	39 07	267	45 14	291	49 38	341
131	59 43	044	21 15	098	24 06	156	38 48	207	38 08	267	44 19	291	49 18	340
132	60 24	042	22 13	098	24 30	156	38 21	207	37 09	267	43 24	290	48 57	338
133	61 03	041	23 12	098	24 54	156	37 54	208	36 10	267	42 28	290	48 34	337
134	61 41	039	24 10	098	25 17	157	37 26	208	35 11	267	41 33	289	48 11	336
	Dubhe		Denebola		•SPICA		ACRUX		•CANOPUS		SIRIUS		•POLLUX	
135	14 17	014	41 33	060	25 09	098	25 41	157	36 58	209	56 25	255	47 46	335
136	14 31	014	42 24	059	26 07	098	26 04	157	36 30	209	55 28	255	47 21	334
137	14 45	014	43 15	059	27 06	097	26 27	157	36 01	210	54 31	255	46 54	333
138	14 59	013	44 05	058	28 05	097	26 49	158	35 32	210	53 33	255	46 26	331
139	15 12	013	44 55	057	29 03	097	27 12	158	35 02	210	52 36	256	45 58	330
140	15 25	012	45 45	057	30 02	097	27 34	158	34 32	211	51 39	256	45 28	329
141	15 37	012	46 34	056	31 00	097	27 55	159	34 01	211	50 42	256	44 57	328
142	15 49	011	47 23	055	31 59	097	28 17	159	33 31	212	49 44	256	44 26	327
143	16 01	011	48 11	054	32 58	097	28 38	159	32 59	212	48 47	256	43 54	326
144	16 11	010	48 59	054	33 56	097	28 59	160	32 28	212	47 50	256	43 20	325
145	16 22	010	49 46	053	34 55	097	29 19	160	31 56	213	46 52	256	42 46	324
146	16 32	010	50 33	052	35 54	097	29 40	160	31 24	213	45 55	256	42 12	324
147	16 42	009	51 19	051	36 53	096	29 59	161	30 52	213	44 58	256	41 36	323
148	16 51	009	52 04	050	37 51	096	30 19	161	30 19	214	44 00	256	41 00	322
149	16 59	008	52 49	049	38 50	096	30 38	161	29 46	214	43 03	256	40 23	321
	Dubhe		ARCTURUS		•SPICA		ACRUX		•CANOPUS		SIRIUS		•POLLUX	
150	17 07	008	20 44	065	39 49	096	30 57	162	29 13	214	42 05	256	39 46	320
151	17 15	007	21 37	065	40 47	096	31 15	162	28 40	215	41 08	257	39 08	319
152	17 22	007	22 31	064	41 46	096	31 33	162	28 06	215	40 10	257	38 29	319
153	17 29	006	23 24	064	42 45	096	31 51	163	27 33	215	39 13	257	37 49	318
154	17 35	006	24 17	063	43 44	096	32 08	163	26 59	215	38 15	257	37 10	317
155	17 41	005	25 09	063	44 43	096	32 25	164	26 24	215	37 18	257	36 29	316
156	17 46	005	26 02	063	45 41	096	32 41	164	25 50	216	36 20	257	35 48	316
157	17 51	004	26 54	062	46 40	096	32 57	165	25 15	216	35 23	257	35 07	315
158	17 55	004	27 47	062	47 39	096	33 12	165	24 41	216	34 25	257	34 25	314
159	17 59	003	28 39	061	48 38	095	33 27	165	24 06	216	33 28	257	33 42	314
160	18 02	003	29 30	061	49 37	095	33 42	166	23 31	216	32 31	256	32 59	313
161	18 04	002	30 22	061	50 35	095	33 56	166	22 55	217	31 33	256	32 16	313
162	18 07	002	31 13	060	51 34	095	34 10	167	22 20	217	30 36	256	31 32	312
163	18 08	001	32 04	060	52 33	095	34 23	167	21 45	217	29 38	256	30 48	311
164	18 09	001	32 55	059	53 32	095	34 36	168	21 09	217	28 41	256	30 04	311
	Dubhe		•ARCTURUS		SPICA		•ACRUX		Suhail		SIRIUS		•POLLUX	
165	18 10	000	33 46	059	54 31	095	34 48	168	48 38	211	27 43	256	29 19	310
166	18 10	000	34 36	058	55 30	095	35 00	169	48 07	212	26 46	256	28 34	310
167	18 10	359	35 26	058	56 29	095	35 11	169	47 35	213	25 49	256	27 48	309
168	18 09	359	36 16	057	57 27	095	35 21	170	47 03	213	24 51	256	27 02	309
169	18 07	358	37 05	056	58 26	095	35 31	170	46 30	214	23 54	256	26 16	308
170	18 05	358	37 54	056	59 25	095	35 41	171	45 57	215	22 57	256	25 29	308
171	18 03	357	38 43	055	60 24	095	35 50	171	45 23	216	21 59	256	24 42	307
172	18 00	357	39 31	055	61 23	095	35 59	172	44 48	216	21 02	256	23 55	307
173	17 56	356	40 19	054	62 22	095	36 07	172	44 13	217	20 05	256	23 08	306
174	17 52	356	41 07	053	63 21	095	36 14	173	43 37	217	19 07	256	22 20	306
175	17 48	355	41 54	053	64 20	095	36 21	174	43 01	218	18 10	256	21 33	306
176	17 43	355	42 41	052	65 18	095	36 27	174	42 25	218	17 13	255	20 44	305
177	17 38	354	43 27	051	66 17	095	36 33	175	41 48	219	16 16	255	19 56	305
178	17 32	354	44 13	050	67 16	095	36 38	175	41 11	219	15 19	255	19 07	305
179	17 25	353	44 58	049	68 15	095	36 43	176	40 33	220	14 21	255	18 19	304

Table 10. A page from AP3270 Sight Reduction Tables for Air Navigation Volume I.

6 Sun sights

For many yacht navigators Sun sights form the guts of the whole business. They are taken during the forenoon or afternoon; a forenoon sight produces a position line which, when 'run up' along the course line to the noon latitude, will give a running fix to supply a noon position. Similarly, the noon latitude can be advanced to the PL produced by the afternoon sight to give a running fix later in the day. The afternoon PL can also be transferred back to the noon latitude to check the noon position.

This system is called 'Sun-run-Sun' and can be operated effectively in quite poor weather conditions. A good navigator needs only a glimpse of the Sun to achieve an altitude. The limitations of the method are obvious. We all know the inaccuracies of the running fix from our efforts along the coast. Also, you can only have one noon fix per day. While it is possible to transfer one Sun PL up to another taken quite soon afterwards, the small change in their angles means that the resulting 'cut' of the PLs

will be very poor. In general, a forenoon sight should be taken not less than one and a half hours before noon. How much earlier you take it will be a trade-off. The earlier the better for the cut of the position lines, but this will mean a longer run-up for the transferred position line to the noon latitude. The longer the run, the bigger the error, particularly if the current is in doubt. Despite these reservations, a good Sun sight is a very useful thing to have, particularly when the stars and planets are obscured by cloud, or you expect a landfall before dusk.

In Chapter 5 we found that what was needed to plot a sight, any sight, was an *assumed* position, an *azimuth* and an *intercept*.

Sight reduction

You will almost certainly be reducing your sights using sight reduction tables. These come in either a marine form running to several volumes, or a condensed version officially for aviators which gets the number of books down

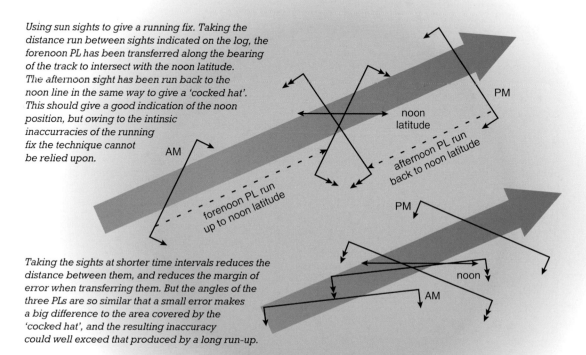

Using sun sights to give a running fix. Taking the distance run between sights indicated on the log, the forenoon PL has been transferred along the bearing of the track to intersect with the noon latitude. The afternoon sight has been run back to the noon line in the same way to give a 'cocked hat'. This should give a good indication of the noon position, but owing to the intinsic inaccuracies of the running fix the technique cannot be relied upon.

AM

noon latitude

PM

forenoon PL run up to noon latitude

afternoon PL run back to noon latitude

PM

noon

AM

Taking the sights at shorter time intervals reduces the distance between them, and reduces the margin of error when transferring them. But the angles of the three PLs are so similar that a small error makes a big difference to the area covered by the 'cocked hat', and the resulting inaccuracy could well exceed that produced by a long run-up.

to three. The latter are more economical to buy and take up less room on board. They are nominally slightly less accurate than the marine equivalent, but since this results from the air tables rounding up or down for decimals of minutes of declination, it is a simple matter to make up this deficiency by interpolation if it really worries you. The business of sight reduction is dealt with in this book on the basis of the *Sight Reduction Tables for Air Navigation* (AP 3270 in the UK, or Pub. No.249 in the US). Volume 1 deals with stars, while volumes 2 and 3 handle all celestial bodies with a declination of less than 30°. This encompasses everything in the solar system: the Moon, the planets and, needless to say, the Sun itself.

Calculators

It is possible to buy pre-programmed navigation calculators loaded with almanac information as well as complete sight reduction data. These remarkable pieces of kit will reduce your sights and give azimuth and intercept from a DR or an assumed position. The advantages are obvious, but it is recommended that before relying upon them as a primary tool, the following simple methods based on tables are mastered. In any case, it would be foolish to go to sea without an almanac and a set of sight reduction tables, lest all else should fail.

THE ASSUMED POSITION

Assumed latitude

You can rarely reduce a sight using your DR latitude because the sight reduction tables will only give you altitudes and azimuths from positions whose latitudes are *whole numbers*. The first thing to do then, is shift your DR latitude to the nearest whole degree. This is called the *assumed latitude*.

Assumed longitude

Next, doctor your DR longitude so that the LHA of the Sun for the time of your sight turns out to be a whole number as well. The reason for this is that, once again, the tables will tolerate no fractions of degrees of LHA.

Now work out the GHA for the Sun at the time of your sight and then, if in west longitude, juggle your DR so that the minutes and decimals are the same as those of the Sun's GHA. When you subtract the longitude from the GHA they will disappear. (See page 11: Local Hour Angle.)

In east longitude, you adjust the minutes of longitude so that when added to the minutes and seconds of the Sun's GHA they add up to a whole number. It's as simple as that.

Example 1: DR longitude 17° 46′W

Sun's GHA at 04h 12m 07s	242°	57′	.3
- Assumed longitude west	17°	57′	.3
LHA	225°		

Example 2: DR longitude 27° 49′E

Sun's GHA at 04h 12m 07s	242°	57′	.3
+ Assumed longitude east	28°	02′	.7
LHA	271°		

AZIMUTH AND INTERCEPT

A working page from Volume 3 of AP 3270 will be found on page 37. Notice that the top right-hand corner gives the latitude 49°. There is a different set of pages for each latitude. Which page of the set you choose is decided by the top central legend, which in this case reads 'Declin-ation (15°-29°) SAME name as latitude'. This means that to choose the right page you need to know the declination of the Sun (obtained from *The Nautical Almanac*) as well as your assumed latitude.

On the extreme left and right of the page are columns showing LHA. Choose the value your assumed position has given and move across into the page until you reach the correct column for your declination (shown in the boxes at top and bottom of the page). You will see that three figures are given, labelled 'Hc', 'd' and 'Z'.

Azimuth

'Z' is the figure from which you find the Sun's azimuth (Zn). The formula for doing this is to be found at the top and bottom left-hand corners of the page - north latitudes at the top, and south latitudes at the bottom, as follows:

N.Lat	LHA greater than 180°...	Zn=Z
	LHA less than 180°...	Zn=360 - Z
S.Lat	LHA greater than 180°...	Zn=180 - Z
	LHA less than 180°...	Zn=180 + Z

Azimuths are, of course, always expressed in degrees True.

Calculated altitude

'Hc' is the calculated altitude for the *whole degree* of declination. To adjust this for minutes of declination take the figure given under 'd'. Using this figure you enter the 'bookmark' table 5 (see page 38). With 'd' as one argument and 'minutes of declination' as the other, extract the value you require and use it to adjust the main figure for Hc. Notice that 'd' is labelled + or – in the main tables. You now have a calculated altitude.

Example

What is the calculated altitude and azimuth for a body whose declination at the time of the sight was 24° 19', whose local hour angle is 315° and which was observed from an assumed latitude of 49°N?

Find the LHA (on the right-hand side of the table) and move across to the column marked 24°. This gives you the following:

Hc 46 57   d + 44   Z 109

Since you are in northern latitudes and the LHA is greater than 180°, Zn=Z. So the azimuth (Zn) is 109°.

As for the calculated altitude, you need to go to the 'bookmark' (page 35). Find 44 in the 'd' column down the side, and move across to the figure in the column beneath the figure 19 (remember that the declination is 24° 19'). This gives you 14, and since the 'd' figure is +44 the resulting increment is + 14.

Hc	46° 57'
d + 44	14'
Hc	47° 11'

You now have an *assumed position* and an *azimuth*. By finding the difference between the calculated altitude above and your observed (corrected sextant) altitude, you have an *intercept* as well.

PRODUCING A SUN SIGHT

1 Put your pro-forma ready on the chart table (see opposite). After you've crossed the Atlantic once, you won't need it any more, but it will help a lot in the early days.
2 Go up on deck, take a sight of the Sun, time it and then read the log. Make sure the time is right because every four seconds can give an error of up to one mile.
3 Fill in 'watch time' in the pro-forma. Correct for GMT.
4 Extract the Sun's GHA and declination for the hour concerned from the daily pages of *The Nautical Almanac*. Enter them in the pro-forma.
5 Work up the actual declination for the minute of the sight, using the 'd' correction if you need to (see page 11). Round any decimals up or down.
6 Turn to the increments pages of the almanac for the minutes and seconds of GHA (see page 32) and enter them in the pro-forma. Work up the Sun's GHA (see page 9).
7 Decide on a suitable assumed longitude and

enter it so as to come up with an LHA for the Sun as a whole number of degrees (see page 41). While you are about it, decide on your assumed latitude and enter it. This will give you your assumed position.
8 Open your sight reduction tables (AP 3270). Check that you have the right page with reference to your assumed latitude, the 'name' of the Sun's declination etc. Extract 'Hc', 'd' and 'Z' and enter them on the pro-forma. Take care to note the sign of 'd'. Is it + or – ?
9 While Ap 3270 is open, check what to do with 'Z' to convert it to 'Zn', and thereby provide you with an azimuth (see page 41). Enter this in the pro-forma.
10 Consult the 'bookmark' Table 5 in AP 3270 to deal with the minutes of declination (see page 41). Enter the answer and then work up the final, corrected, calculated altitude (Hc).
11 Enter your sextant reading in the pro-forma. Enter the index error (if any) and dip, (see page 17) then work up the apparent altitude. Extract the altitude correction from the 'bookmark' of The Nautical Almanac (the left-hand table), enter it and work up the true altitude (Ho).
12 Compare this with Hc; the difference is your intercept (see page 28). Label it towards or away, and you have all you need to plot your sight (see Chapter 5).

USING THE SIGHT

If you take a forenoon sight like this at about 0930 local time and then run it up to your noon latitude by transferring the position line along your course line the appropriate number of miles, you will have a fix at the point where the transferred position line cuts the latitude (see page 40).

You can check this by taking another observation in the afternoon, between 1400 and 1500 local time, and then running the PL back. See what sort of cocked hat you produce and evaluate the result. In good conditions you could expect to achieve an area of probable position two to four miles across. You may do much better - but remember, at best this is only a running fix.

Sorting the good from the bad

The more experienced you are, the easier it is to assess the quality of a particular sight. If you are in doubt about the standard of an important one, and if conditions and time available for navigation permit, take a series of observations (five or seven is customary) and graph the results, time against altitude.

PRO-FORMA FOR SUN SIGHT

Date **1 MAY 1986**

DR **49° 12' N**
5° 10' W

Watch time	**09 15 23**
Correction	**FAST −6**
GMT	**09h 15m 17s**

GHA (hrs)	**315° 43'.4**
+Correction (mins/secs)	**3 49.3**
GHA	**319 32.7**
Assumed Long	**5 32.7**
LHA	**314°**

Assumed Lat **49° N**

Hc	**39 28**	z	**116**	Declination (hrs) **15 02.1N**
d **+47**	**+2**	~~180/360~~		d difference **07** **+0.2**
Hc	**39° 30'**	Zn	**116**	Declination **15° 02'.3N**

Hs	**39° 28**
Index Error	**− −**
Dip **8 FEET**	**−02.7**
Apparent Alt	**39 25.3**
Main Correction	**+14.8**
Ho	**39 40.1**
Hc	**39 30**
Intercept	**10.1** TOWARDS/~~AWAY~~

Use the blank proforma on page 64 for your own working.

The good sights should produce a reasonably straight line. Any duffers can be thrown out, and a time and altitude average taken for those which remain. That is the value to use in your workings.

At this point, let me remind you that most difficulties and errors arise from carelessness in looking things up or in reading the sextant. Keep a firm grip on your head. Go one step at a time and every sight will be a winner.

Now try it

1st May 1986. You take a forenoon sight at 09h 15m 23s watch time. The sextant altitude was 39° 28' and the log read 206.4. Your height of eye was estimated to be eight feet, your watch was six seconds fast and your sextant has no index error. Your DR position was 49° 12'N 5° 10'W. At noon the log reads 218.9 and you observe your latitude to be 49° 15.5. You have been steering 085°T and the tide has cancelled itself out. Plot your position line.

You will find the working and the finished plot below. Don't look at it now; use it to check your own efforts. Working through an example like this is the best way to learn, and with a subject like celestial navigation it is probably the *only* way.

This chapter on Sun sights is very important. In many ways it forms the basis for most of the subsequent chapters, so make sure you understand it thoroughly before standing on any further.

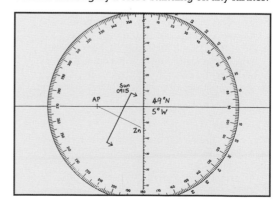

7 The planets

Of the various planets in the solar system, only Venus, Mars, Jupiter and Saturn are useful to the navigator. If they are available for observation they will be clearly visible at twilight, morning or evening. The planets burn so brightly that once you have worked out where one is likely to be, it is extremely easy to identify. The method for reducing your observation to a position line is very similar to that used for the Sun.

TWILIGHT

If you want to measure the altitude of any heavenly body you need a horizon. At night there is generally no horizon and in the daytime you can't see the stars and planets, so the time to observe them is *twilight*.

In practice, the time span of twilight is obvious. In the evening it starts when you see the first planet or star appear and ends when you can no longer discern a horizon. In the morning, it begins as the horizon firms up into a line and ends when the brightest star disappears.

This period, depending on season and latitude, is generally within 20 minutes (plus or minus) of the time of *civil twilight* which is tabulated for various latitudes on the daily pages of *The Nautical Almanac*.

If you are pre-computing the approximate position of a planet, and certainly when you come to work out which star is which (see Chapter 9), you will need to know the time of civil twilight for your rough position.

Don't get bogged down with 'nautical twilight', since it is not relevant to your calculations. Just look up the time of civil twilight (CT) in the almanac, make a mental interpolation for latitude, and you will have it in GMT for the Greenwich Meridian. A quick arc-to-time calculation will adjust this for your own longitude.

Example
May 3rd 1986. What time approximately is civil twilight in the morning at DR 22°N 55°W? See page 31. Interpolating between 20°N and 30°N, civil twilight on the Greenwich Meridian at 22°N is 0504 GMT. Since the Sun is moving towards the west, twilight will be later in 55° west longitude by 55 x 4 minutes = 220 minutes = 3h 40 minutes. Therefore civil twilight is at 0844 GMT at our position.

PLANET IDENTIFICATION

There is a fine description of the planets and their movements in *The Nautical Almanac* which tells you which planet is likely to be where. You may also find the data in other sources, but the most accurate method for finding a planet is as follows.

Extract the time of civil twilight and then, using a planet pro-forma, enter this time as the time of an observation. Working from this, consult the almanac to find an approximate LHA, assumed latitude and declination for the planet concerned (you can be very rough) and enter the sight reduction tables. These will give you a calculated altitude and an azimuth. Don't bother to correct the calculated altitude for minutes of declination.

At twilight, sight along the azimuth and look up to something like the calculated altitude. The bright star there is your planet.

Once you have a planet well and truly recognised you can, in all probability, use it for the rest of the voyage. They don't change their position very rapidly so you don't have to go through this every day.

It is said that with careful pre-computing you can find Venus in your sextant telescope during the day and so take a sight of it. Bright though it undoubtedly is, I have had no luck with this one. You might like to try it all the same because it could be extremely useful. I'm still working on it myself...

SHOOTING A PLANET OR STAR

Having identified your planet you'll find shooting it is easier than the Sun. There is always a hint of doubt about when the Sun's lower limb is perfectly on the horizon, but a star or planet is just a point source of light. It is either on the horizon or it isn't. Pull it down, give the sextant wrist a quick pendulum

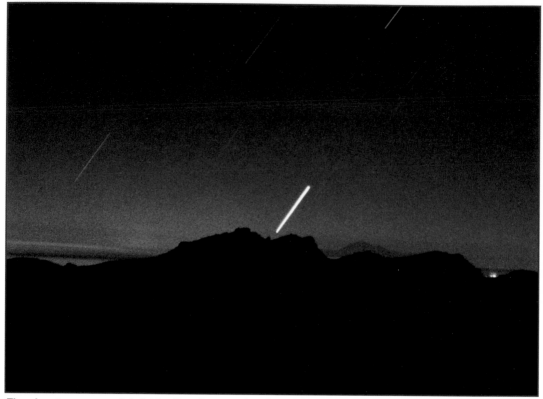

The planets are so much brighter than the stars that they are easy to identify and can be seen when the sky is quite bright. This is Venus rising (time-lapse photography).

twist to ensure you are perpendicular, and note the time.

PLANET SIGHT REDUCTION

A study of the planet pro-forma will show that the system for working out a planet sight is virtually identical to that used for the Sun. There are, however, a few small differences.

The 'v' correction for GHA
This is an extra incremental correction for the GHA of a planet. You will find 'v' alongside 'd' at the bottom of the daily page column for your planet in the almanac. You apply it to GHA in the same way that you apply 'd' for declination. You can look it up at the same time as you check your GHA minutes and seconds increment. Notice that it is not always positive. For Venus, for example, 'v' is sometimes negative - so watch out.

Apparent altitude and parallax
As with the Sun, you have to apply an apparent altitude correction to your sextant altitude after

dealing with index error and dip. You will find the correction in the centre of the bookmark page of the almanac. The figure is much smaller for stars and planets than for the Sun. This is because it contains no correction for semi-diameter.

Don't forget that Mars and Venus may have an additional small correction for parallax (see page 18). This can be found alongside the apparent altitude correction on the bookmark page. Apply it below the apparent altitude correction in the sextant corrections on the pro-forma.

Example
May 1st 1986. You are in DR 49°N 35° 30'W and you observe Venus through the sextant telescope at 20h 15m 18s watch time. Your watch is set to GMT, and is 10 seconds slow. Sextant altitude is 33° 13'.6, index error is 2.8' on the arc and you estimate your height of eye to be 12 feet. Plot your position line.

The completed pro-forma and plot are illustrated overleaf - but see if you can do it yourself first.

PRO-FORMA FOR PLANET SIGHT

Date	**1 MAY 1986**		Watch time	20 15 18
Planet	**VENUS**		Correction	+10
DR	**49°N 35° 30' W**		GMT	20 15 28

GHA (hrs)	95 19.9	
+Correction (mins/secs)	3 52.0	
v **(−0.8)**	−0.2	
GHA	99 11.7	
Assumed Long	35 11.7 W	Assumed Lat **49°N**
LHA	64°	

Hc	**33 19**	z	**94**	Declination (hrs)	22 02.3N
d **(+43)**	+2	180/360	360−94	d **(0·6+)**	+0.2
Ic	**33 21**	Zn	**266**	Declination	22 02.5N

Hs	33 13·6
Index Error	−2·8
Dip	−3·4
Apparent Alt	33 07·4
Correction	−01·5
Parallax	+00·1
Ho	33 06
Hc	33 21
Intercept	15 AWAY

That is all there is to planet sights. They can be useful on their own, and can often form part of a set of star and planet sights for a good fix at twilight. You can also make them part of a running fix by transferring an afternoon Sun PL up to an evening planet PL, or transferring a morning planet PL up to the forenoon Sun sight.

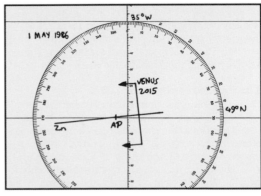

8 The Moon

Traditionally, while the Moon has delighted poets down the ages, it has not been the navigator's favourite body. This is because it requires just a little extra effort to reduce a Moon sight and therefore leaves more room for the careless to come unstuck. 'The Moon is inaccurate', they howl, shaking their fists at it. The Moon is no such thing. All its movements are ordered and they are all tabulated in the almanac. It's up to you, mate, what you make of it.

The wonderful thing about the Moon is that it is often visible at the same time as the Sun and at a reasonable angular distance from it. This gives you the opportunity to take *simultaneous sights* and achieve a real fix, albeit a two-point one.

'Simultaneous' means, in this context, taking two or more sights within such a short time that you do not have to bother about how far you have run between them. If you are doing five knots and you take two sights five minutes apart, your change of position isn't going to make a lot of difference to the results.

Generally the Moon is usefully available for observation a few days before and after half Moon, both waxing and waning, but it also offers itself at other times.

CORRECTIONS IN SIGHT REDUCTION

As a basic proposition, the closer the target to Earth, the more corrections you will have to make when reducing the sight. The Moon, a mere 250,000 miles away, is particularly susceptible. Its GHA varies a lot from the regular, as does the rate of change in declination. Its closeness also makes horizontal parallax a very real factor when correcting apparent altitude.

Upper and lower limb

Unlike the Sun, which usually presents us with a view of its whole disc, the Moon is frequently partially obscured. In many of its phases you have no choice but to shoot the upper limb. Shooting the 'ghostly galleon' can be pleasant, but often you are stuck with the dreaded inverted melon slice. For some reason this is more difficult to observe accurately.

Horizontal parallax corrections are tabulated for both the upper and lower limb. All other corrections assume that you are taking a lower limb observation. This creates no problems, however, because if you shoot the upper limb you simply subtract 30′ from your corrected altitude and that takes care of the matter.

THE MOON SIGHT PRO-FORMA

When you refer to the Moon in the daily pages of the almanac (see page 31) you will see that there are five columns of information. GHA we know about, and 'v' is just the same as for the planets: it is the increment by which the GHA varies from the regular. Because this changes so frequently in the case of the Moon, it warrants a column of its own. Note that the Moon also has its own column in the increment tables for minutes and seconds of time for GHA as well.

Declination is self-explanatory and 'd', the increment correction, is treated like 'v' because of its rapid variations.

The only newcomer is the horizontal parallax (HP) column. You will find a space on the pro-forma for 'HP' in the altitude corrections, because HP (see page 14) represents an error in the observed altitude.

All these values are entered into the pro-forma (see page 49). Note that 'v' is always *added* to the GHA because the Moon rises later each day.

Like all declination increments, 'd' may be added or subtracted. Find out which by inspection of the hours adjacent to the one you are interested in. If the declination is increasing by the hour, then the 'd' value is positive. If it is decreasing, then it is negative.

Everything else is straightforward until you come to the *altitude*.

ALTITUDE CORRECTION TABLES FOR THE MOON

These are to be found at the very back of the almanac. They are easy enough to follow and the system described in the tables leaves no doubt

App. Alt.	0°–4° Corrⁿ	5°–9° Corrⁿ	10°–14° Corrⁿ	15°–19° Corrⁿ	20°–24° Corrⁿ	25°–29° Corrⁿ	30°–34° Corrⁿ	App. Alt.
00	0° 33·8	5° 58·2	10° 62·1	15° 62·8	20° 62·2	25° 60·8	30° 58·9	00
10	35·9	58·5	62·2	62·8	62·1	60·8	58·8	10
20	37·8	58·7	62·2	62·8	62·1	60·7	58·8	20
30	39·6	58·9	62·3	62·8	62·1	60·7	58·7	30
40	41·2	59·1	62·3	62·8	62·0	60·6	58·6	40
50	42·6	59·3	62·4	62·7	62·0	60·6	58·5	50
00	1° 44·0	6° 59·5	11° 62·4	16° 62·7	21° 62·0	26° 60·5	31° 58·5	00
10	45·2	59·7	62·4	62·7	61·9	60·4	58·4	10
20	46·3	59·9	62·5	62·7	61·9	60·4	58·3	20
30	47·3	60·0	62·5	62·7	61·9	60·3	58·2	30
40	48·3	60·2	62·5	62·7	61·8	60·3	58·2	40
50	49·2	60·3	62·6	62·7	61·8	60·2	58·1	50
00	2° 50·0	7° 60·5	12° 62·6	17° 62·7	22° 61·7	27° 60·1	32° 58·0	00
10	50·8	60·6	62·6	62·6	61·7	60·1	57·9	10
20	51·4	60·7	62·6	62·6	61·6	60·0	57·8	20
30	52·1	60·9	62·7	62·6	61·6	59·9	57·8	30
40	52·7	61·0	62·7	62·6	61·5	59·9	57·7	40
50	53·3	61·1	62·7	62·6	61·5	59·8	57·6	50
00	3° 53·8	8° 61·2	13° 62·7	18° 62·5	23° 61·5	28° 59·7	33° 57·5	00
10	54·3	61·3	62·7	62·5	61·4	59·7	57·4	10
20	54·8	61·4	62·7	62·5	61·4	59·6	57·4	20
30	55·2	61·5	62·8	62·5	61·3	59·6	57·3	30
40	55·6	61·6	62·8	62·4	61·3	59·5	57·2	40
50	56·0	61·6	62·8	62·4	61·2	59·4	57·1	50
00	4° 56·4	9° 61·7	14° 62·8	19° 62·4	24° 61·2	29° 59·3	34° 57·0	00
10	56·7	61·8	62·8	62·3	61·1	59·3	56·9	10
20	57·1	61·9	62·8	62·3	61·1	59·2	56·9	20
30	57·4	61·9	62·8	62·3	61·0	59·1	56·8	30
40	57·7	62·0	62·8	62·2	60·9	59·1	56·7	40
50	57·9	62·1	62·8	62·2	60·9	59·0	56·6	50

H.P.	L　U	L　U	L　U	L　U	L　U	L　U	L　U	H.P.
54·0	0·3 0·9	0·3 0·9	0·4 1·0	0·5 1·1	0·6 1·2	0·7 1·3	0·9 1·5	54·0
54·3	0·7 1·1	0·7 1·2	0·7 1·2	0·8 1·3	0·9 1·4	1·1 1·5	1·2 1·7	54·3
54·6	1·1 1·4	1·1 1·4	1·1 1·4	1·2 1·5	1·3 1·6	1·4 1·7	1·5 1·8	54·6
54·9	1·4 1·6	1·5 1·6	1·5 1·6	1·6 1·7	1·6 1·8	1·8 1·9	1·9 2·0	54·9
55·2	1·8 1·8	1·8 1·8	1·9 1·9	1·9 1·9	2·0 2·0	2·1 2·1	2·2 2·2	55·2
55·5	2·2 2·0	2·2 2·0	2·3 2·1	2·3 2·1	2·4 2·2	2·4 2·3	2·5 2·4	55·5
55·8	2·6 2·2	2·6 2·2	2·6 2·3	2·7 2·3	2·7 2·4	2·8 2·4	2·9 2·5	55·8
56·1	3·0 2·4	3·0 2·5	3·0 2·5	3·0 2·5	3·1 2·6	3·1 2·6	3·2 2·7	56·1
56·4	3·4 2·7	3·4 2·7	3·4 2·7	3·4 2·7	3·4 2·8	3·5 2·8	3·5 2·9	56·4
56·7	3·7 2·9	3·7 2·9	3·8 2·9	3·8 2·9	3·8 3·0	3·8 3·0	3·9 3·0	56·7
57·0	4·1 3·1	4·1 3·1	4·1 3·1	4·1 3·1	4·2 3·1	4·2 3·2	4·2 3·2	57·0
57·3	4·5 3·3	4·5 3·3	4·5 3·3	4·5 3·3	4·5 3·3	4·5 3·4	4·6 3·4	57·3
57·6	4·9 3·5	4·9 3·5	4·9 3·5	4·9 3·5	4·9 3·5	4·9 3·5	4·9 3·6	57·6
57·9	5·3 3·8	5·3 3·8	5·2 3·8	5·2 3·7	5·2 3·7	5·2 3·7	5·2 3·7	57·9
58·2	5·6 4·0	5·6 4·0	5·6 4·0	5·6 4·0	5·6 3·9	5·6 3·9	5·6 3·9	58·2
58·5	6·0 4·2	6·0 4·2	6·0 4·2	6·0 4·2	6·0 4·1	5·9 4·1	5·9 4·1	58·5
58·8	6·4 4·4	6·4 4·4	6·4 4·4	6·3 4·4	6·3 4·3	6·3 4·3	6·2 4·2	58·8
59·1	6·8 4·6	6·8 4·6	6·7 4·6	6·7 4·6	6·7 4·5	6·6 4·5	6·6 4·4	59·1
59·4	7·2 4·8	7·1 4·8	7·1 4·8	7·1 4·8	7·0 4·7	7·0 4·7	6·9 4·6	59·4
59·7	7·5 5·0	7·5 5·0	7·5 5·0	7·5 5·0	7·4 4·9	7·3 4·8	7·2 4·7	59·7
60·0	7·9 5·3	7·9 5·3	7·9 5·2	7·8 5·2	7·8 5·1	7·7 5·0	7·6 4·9	60·0
60·3	8·3 5·5	8·3 5·5	8·2 5·4	8·2 5·4	8·1 5·3	8·0 5·2	7·9 5·1	60·3
60·6	8·7 5·7	8·7 5·7	8·6 5·7	8·6 5·6	8·5 5·5	8·4 5·4	8·2 5·3	60·6
60·9	9·1 5·9	9·0 5·9	9·0 5·9	8·9 5·8	8·8 5·7	8·7 5·6	8·5 5·4	60·9
61·2	9·5 6·2	9·4 6·1	9·4 6·1	9·3 6·0	9·2 5·9	9·1 5·8	8·9 5·6	61·2
61·5	9·8 6·4	9·8 6·3	9·7 6·3	9·7 6·2	9·5 6·1	9·4 5·9	9·2 5·8	61·5

One of the altitude correction tables for the Moon from the end of the Nautical Almanac.

about how this should be done. So 'when all else fails, read the instructions'. They even give you a 'dip' table on the same page so that you don't have to scrabble through the book looking for the one you use for everything else.

Correct your sextant altitude for index error and dip just as you would for any other sight. This gives you your apparent altitude.

There are now two corrections to apply. The *first correction* is found in the upper section of the altitude correction tables for the Moon. It is straightforward enough, but is set out in a rather unusual manner. The only argument for entry into the table is apparent altitude. Here are two examples to help you familiarise yourself with it.

Example 1

Your apparent altitude is 12° 20′.
What is the first correction?
Find 12° (one of the bold figures in the body of the table), then go down the adjacent column until you find the correction figure opposite 20′ in the **App Alt** column. The answer is 62.6′

Example 2

Your apparent altitude is 34° 37′. What is the first correction?
The answer is 56.7′.

The *second correction* will refer to horizontal parallax (HP) which you extract from the fifth 'Moon' column of the daily page in the almanac and note on your pro-forma. The Moon altitude correction table is entered with HP as your argument (side columns). Move across the table until you are in the column from which you took the first correction for apparent altitude. 'L' and 'U' refer to the upper and lower limb and you can choose accordingly.

Example 3

What are corrections 1 and 2 for an apparent altitude of 25° 42′ and an HP figure of 56.4? The sight was of the Moon's lower limb.
Correction 1 is 60.6.
Correction 2 is 3.5, obtained by dropping straight down the column from correction 1 and selecting the sub-column headed L′.

Both corrections are added to the apparent altitude and when applied give the true altitude (Ho) for the Moon's *lower* limb. If you observed the *upper* limb, you'll have to subtract 30′ from the result, as in the third

PRO-FORMA FOR MOON SIGHT

Date **1 MAY 1986**

DR: 41°S 25° 38'E

Watch time	**10 1409**	
Correction		
GMT	**10 1409**	

GHA (hrs)	**50° 45.9**	
+ Correction (mins/secs)	**3 22.6**	
+ v **(09.2)**	**2.2**	
GHA	**54 10.7**	
Assumed Long	**25 49.3E**	Assumed Lat **41°S**
LHA	**80°**	

Hc	**20 57**	z	**80**	Declination (hrs)	**21 27.8 S**
d36	**15**	180/360	**+180**	d **-(10.8)**	**-2.6**
Hc	**21 12**	Zn	**260**	Declination	**21 25.2 S**

	Hs	**20 48.2**
	Index Error	**-1 ON**
	Dip	**-3.4**
	Apparent Alt	**20 43.8**
	+ 1st correction	**62.0**
Hp **57.8**	+ 2nd correction	**3.7**
	Ho Lower Limb	**21 49.5**
	3rd Correction	**-0 30.0**
	Ho Upper Limb	**21 19.5**
	Hc	**21 12**
	INTERCEPT	**7.5** TOWARDS/~~AWAY~~

correction on the pro-forma. This compensates for the Moon's diameter.

You now have all the information you need to take a Moon sight.

Example 4

May 1st, 1986. You are in DR 41° S 25° 38'E and are able to observe the Moon's upper limb. The time is 10h 14m 09s GMT (you have just adjusted your watch) and the sextant altitude was 20° 48.2. Index error is 1' on the arc and your height of eye is about 12 feet. Plot your position line. The worked pro-forma and plot are shown here, but as before, see if you can figure out the answer yourself.

If you use your pro-forma as a guide and work through it step by step, Moon sight reduction should not prove a problem. If, however, you are struggling to cope with the Moon's eccentricities, leave it alone for a while and

go on to the stars. These are the easiest of the lot to reduce and, as you'll see, simple to identify. You will find that they are of immense importance to your navigation.

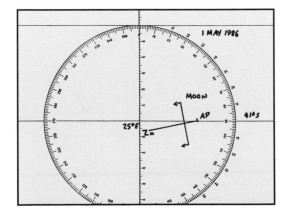

9 The stars

Most people who dabble in celestial navigation are under the mistaken impression that star sights are a problem. This misconception arises from two great fallacies:

1 It is difficult to identify the star you want because it is twilight and the constellations are invisible, and you would be involved in an unacceptable amount of rote learning to memorise all the names.

2 Working out star sights is complicated and plotting is a nightmare.

These objections are complete nonsense, and here's why:

1 You don't personally have to identify the star you require because Volume 1 of AP 3270 does it for you. The arithmetic needed to extract the information can be readily handled by a ten-year-old.

Like many of us, you may choose to identify the stars by name for your own satisfaction. If the night is bright and it's your watch, what better way can there be of keeping awake to your place in the universe than kitting yourself up with a well-laced coffee and a star map, and watching the stars in their courses. The names are as beautiful as the starts themselves: Aldebaran, Sirius, Procyon and the rest. While you are out there, treat yourself to a look into the Pleiades or the nebula in the Sword of Orion with your ship's binoculars. As the sky leaps into 3-D, it is like peering down the throat of infinity. However, if all this fails to turn you on, stick with the simple arithmetic. It won't let you down.

2 Working out sights and plotting them is like every other job - building a boat, climbing a mountain, or even installing central heating. If you squint up the hill from the beginning to the end result, it is a daunting prospect, but if you take the task as a series of small stages leading towards completion, you will overcome the psychological barrier with ease. Indeed, if you reconsider the apparently complicated star pro-forma you'll realise that it is actually the simplest of all.

Just as a guide, a competent navigator working with a mate to note the times of the observations can shoot seven stars in about fifteen minutes on a good evening. It will then take another half hour or so to reduce and plot them. For less than an hour's pleasant work you can produce a fix which could well be good to a mile or less anywhere on the Earth, using bodies whose distance away from us shivers the brain on its mountings.

Brightness of stars (magnitude)

There are over 4,000 stars visible from Earth, but the vast majority are of no benefit to the navigator. There are 57 which are readily identified and bright enough to be used. These 57 are indexed in the almanac and also on the back of the bookmark page. This gives the name of each star, its magnitude, its SHA (Sidereal Hour Angle), of which more shortly, and its approximate declination.

The magnitude of a star is its brightness. The *higher* the number, the *dimmer* the star. Capella at 0.2 is much brighter than Menkar at 2.8. Sirius is so bright it is off the scale and has the negative value of −1.6. The bigger the negative number, the brighter the star.

No.	Name	Mag.	S.H.A.	Dec.
1	*Alpheratz*	2·2	358	N. 29
2	*Ankaa*	2·4	354	S. 42
3	*Schedar*	2·5	350	N. 56
4	*Diphda*	2·2	349	S. 18
5	*Achernar*	0·6	336	S. 57
6	*Hamal*	2·2	328	N. 23
7	*Acamar*	3·1	316	S. 40
8	*Menkar*	2·8	315	N. 4
9	*Mirfak*	1·9	309	N. 50
10	*Aldebaran*	1·1	291	N. 16
11	*Rigel*	0·3	282	S. 8
12	*Capella*	0·2	281	N. 46
13	*Bellatrix*	1·7	279	N. 6
14	*Elnath*	1·8	279	N. 29
15	*Alnilam*	1·8	276	S. 1
16	Betelgeuse	Var.*	271	N. 7
17	*Canopus*	−0·9	264	S. 53
18	*Sirius*	−1·6	259	S. 17

Part of the index of 57 selected stars.

It is worth noting here that the magnitude of the planets varies and is tabulated in the daily pages of the almanac alongside each planet's name in the top box of the 'planet columns'.

FIRST POINT OF ARIES AND SIDEREAL HOUR ANGLE (SHA)

Because there are so many stars it would be impractical and expensive to tabulate the movements of every one for each day of the year.

Owing to the effectively infinite distance between us and the stars, their positions relative to one another on the celestial sphere do not vary significantly. The declinations of the stars

remain the same throughout the year as the Earth moves round its microscopic orbit, but as it turns beneath them once a day, their GHAs advance with a marvellous regularity. Since the stars are a fixed angular distance apart, their GHAs all proceed at the same rate. So if the movement of just one is tabulated and the angles from this to all the others are known, it is a simple matter to calculate the GHA of any star at a given time.

The point on the celestial sphere from which all the other GHAs are calculated is called the *First Point of Aries* and given the symbol of the ram ♈.

The east-west angle between Aries and the position of a given star is known as the *Sidereal Hour Angle* (SHA) of the star; in other words, the

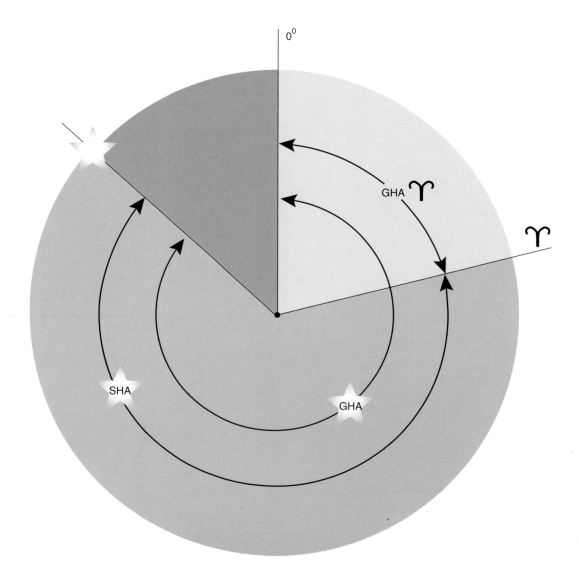

star's SHA is its angular distance to the west of Aries. For example, the GHA of Altair = GHA ♈ + SHA Altair.

If the resulting GHA turns out to be greater than 360°, you should subtract 360 from it to arrive at a workable figure.

If you need to know the exact SHA and declination of a star you will find them tabulated in the daily pages of the almanac, at the right-hand side of the stars and planets half of the double-page daily spread (page 30). They are also set out on the bookmark (page 50), but here they are rounded to the nearest whole number for quick reference.

Example
What is the celestial position (GHA and dec.) of Diphda on May 1st 1988 at 10h 14m 26s?

GHA Aries 18h	129°	22′	.0
+ Increment (page 32)	3°	37′	.1
GHA Aries	132°	59′	.1
+ SHA Diphda	349°	16′	.8
GHA Diphda	482°	15'	.9
— 360	360°		
GHA Diphda	122°	15'	.9

Declination S18°03'.8 (from almanac star tables).

REDUCING A SINGLE STARSIGHT

If the declination of a star is less than 30° then it can be reduced like the Sun or a planet using Volumes 2 or 3 of AP 3270. Work out the GHA of the star from the GHA of Aries and the star's SHA and then proceed. There will be no incremental changes in declination since this is virtually constant.

It is actually quite rare to reduce a starsight like this because of the potential problems of identifying stars and because there is an easier way by using the planned system described below.

Volume 1 of AP 3270 - 'Selected Stars'
When you get hold of a copy of this wonderful book you will see that on the front cover beneath the title it bears the legend, 'Epoch 2000.0'. This edition covers five years either side of 2000. Volumes 2 and 3 go on for as long as you can hold the pages together.

The illustration on page 39 is a reproduction of a working page from AP 3270 Volume 1. Notice the assumed latitude at the top of the page - this time named north or south (in this case south). The argument for entry is LHA of Aries.

Reading across for a given LHA there are seven stars listed, all with their calculated altitude (Hc) and azimuth (Zn), arrayed in ascending order of azimuth. These are the actual values for this LHA. *No further calculation is required.*

The stars whose names are in capital letters are the brightest, and those marked with the symbol ◆ will, when plotted, give the best 'cut' for a fix.

PLANNING A STARSIGHT SESSION

Given a clear twilight in decent weather there is no reason why, with practice, you should not be able to shoot all seven of the stars recommended for your location in Volume 1. The seven chosen are selected for their probable visibility and their viability as sources of good position lines.

Prepare for them all, then. Even if you don't catch the lot because of cloud, weather or plain incompetence, you should get enough for a fix. But, to be in with a chance of any, you need to know where to find them. Here is the big secret...

1 Determine the time of civil twilight for your DR position (see page 44).
2 Work out the LHA of Aries for this time and location. As always, it needs to be a whole number to enter the tables, so choose an assumed longitude accordingly. You can use the top of the starsight pro-forma for this.
3 Open Volume 1 at the page for your latitude and look up the LHA you have calculated. Those are your stars, together with their altitudes and azimuths for your assumed position. For purposes of finding the stars these values will be as effective as the real values from your actual position.
4 You will probably be able to start observing the brighter stars before the official time of civil twilight. In order to do this you simply go back one degree of LHA for four minutes of time. I generally make a note like this, going forward from civil twilight as well to give myself an extra chance at that end.

Time		LHA
1828		132
1832		133
1836		134
1840	——Civil Twilight——	135
1844		136
1848		137
1852		138

5 Have Volume 1 open on the chart table and your note of LHAs and times (see above) beside it. Give the deck watch to your mate and put your pro-forma on the table as well. No doubt you'll improvise if you have only a small chart table.

6 The moment conditions allow (just before the first star comes out in the evening, or as soon as the eastern horizon firms up in the morning) decide on your first star. It is generally more useful to begin with the stars to the east of you and end with those to the west. The eastern horizon sharpens up first in the morning, and in the evening the western horizon stays visible longest. If there is a lot of cloud about, however, common sense must prevail. Grab what you can when you can.

7 Look up the star's altitude for the *current LHA of Aries* and set your sextant to this figure. Then hang your handbearing compass round your neck and nip up on deck. Use the compass to look down the azimuth of the star (don't forget to allow for magnetic variation: azimuths are in degrees True) and 'fix' the direction with a cloud, or star, or ship, or something. If there is nothing, you'll just have to concentrate harder. Then look towards the horizon in that direction through your preset sextant.

8 If all is well the star will appear somewhere in your field of view. Rack it up or down to the horizon and call 'NOW', at which point your mate marks the exact time. You then go back to the chart table and note the time, the sextant angle and the name of the star in your pro-forma. Read your sextant *carefully*, because there's no going back. Once this is done, you can extract the data on the next star and do it again.

You'll be amazed at how well this works. It may be necessary to 'sweep the horizon' to find the star, but usually they appear without much trouble. Pick bright stars to start with. Some of the feeble ones can be a bit demoralising and may need to be abandoned altogether.

If you can't find a particular star, carry on to the next. You have only a short time to shoot the lot and there is none to waste. If you go for seven, you may not get them all but you should have enough for a satisfactory fix. And if there is a nice, fat planet sidling around the sky, pull it down too for good measure. You may not bother to reduce it, but it could be a useful ace if there is ambiguity in your plot. Planets are always a bonus because they are visible when the sky is too bright to see the stars. For this reason you needn't waste any 'star time' shooting them.

Nab them late in the morning, or early in the evening.

DISTANCE RUN BETWEEN STARSIGHTS

We have seen that the great benefit of a set of 'simultaneous' starsights is that the element of a 'run' between sights is removed and the resulting fix can be far more accurate in consequence. Unfortunately, if your boat is sailing at six knots and it takes you 25 minutes to shoot all your stars, she will have travelled two and a half miles through the water between the first and the last sight.

There are two things you can do about this. If you are in no hurry, the best option is to heave to while you make your observations. This will not only stop your boat, it will also considerably reduce her motion and make your job quicker and easier. If you are cursed with a vessel that won't heave to happily, or if you don't want to stop, you should note the log reading at the beginning, the middle and the end of your set of sights. I generally run the early ones up to the middle sight and the last ones back, so that the time of the actual fix is around the centre of the span of your observations. By reference to the various times and your approximate heading, you can make the necessary adjustments to the position lines in your head with an adequate degree of accuracy. There is no need to cover your plot with a network of confusing spider lines.

MULTIPLE STARSIGHT REDUCTION

If you look at the pro-forma for starsight reduction you'll see that it is in two sections. The first half helps you work out the LHA of Aries, so as to be able to pre-compute which stars to observe (see page 51). To use this part of the form you enter the GHA of Aries for the GMT of civil twilight at your position in the box for GHA, followed by its increments of minutes (seconds don't matter here), and carry on from there.

Whilst taking your sights you will have filled in the names of the stars observed, the exact time of each observation and the sextant altitudes. As you complete the other sections you will find that several of them have the same entry 'across the board'; for example, the 'watch time' correction. The GHA of Aries will be the same if all the observations fall in the same hour, but note that the increments for minutes will vary from sight to sight. So will your assumed

longitude because, as with all the other forms for sight reduction, you are going for a whole number of degrees for each LHA of Aries.

Index error can be filled in right across, but watch out for dip. On my boat I have to move around quite a bit to shoot all seven stars. Some I can get from the comfort of the wheel box aft, (height of eye eight feet); for others I have to stand on the bow, (height of eye 13 feet); and it is not unknown for me to be seen lying in the lee scuppers with my sextant on a calm evening looking under the sails with my height of eye down to four feet at the most.

The corrections to apparent altitude are extracted from the centre column of the bookmark of the almanac and the calculated altitude (Hc) and the azimuth come, of course, from Volume 1 of AP 3270. Your assumed

STARSIGHT PRO-FORMA

Date: 1 MAY 1986

Time of CT: 0855 GMT

DR: 10°S 139°E

GHA ♈	338° 57.4
Increment (mins)	13 47.3
GHA ♈	352 44.7
Ass. Long.	138 15.3
LHA ♈	491 = 131 (-360)

Assumed Lat: 10°S

STAR	REGULUS	SPICA	ACRUX	CANOPUS	RIGEL	BETELGEUSE	POLLUX
WATCH TIME CORRECTION	08 54 16 +1	08 56 10 +1	08 46 14 +1	08 50 11 +1	08 52 35 +1	09 00 01 +1	09 06 27 +1
GMT	08 54 17	08 56 11	08 46 15	08 50 12	08 52 36	09 00 02	09 06 28
GHA ♈ INCREMENT	338 57.4 13 36.2	338 57.4 14 05.1	338 57.4 11 35.6	338 57.4 12 35.1	338 57.4 13 11.2	353 59.9 0 00.5	353 59.9 1 37.3
GHA ♈ ASS. LONG.	352 33.6 138 26.4	353 02.5 138 57.5	350 33.0 139 27.0	351 32.5 139 27.5	352 08.6 138 51.4	354 00.4 138 59.6	355 38.2 139 21.8
LHA ♈	491 131	492 132	490 130	491 131	491 131	493 133	495 135
Hs INDEX ERROR DIP	60 13.6 (8') -2.7	22 39.5 (8') -2.7	23 53.9 (12') -3.4	39 05.9 (8') -2.7	37 47.8 (12') -3.4	42 11.5 (8') -2.7	47 04.6 (8') -2.7
APP. ALT. CORRECTION	60 10.9 -0.6	22 36.8 -2.3	23 50.5 -2.2	39 03.2 -1.2	37 44.4 -1.2	42 08.8 -1.1	47 01.9 -0.9
Ho Hc	60 10.3 59 43	22 34.5 22 13	23 48.3 23 41	39 02.0 38 48	37 43.2 38 08	42 07.7 42 28	47 01 47 46
INTERCEPT	27.3 T	21.5 T	7.3 T	14 T	24.8 A	20.3 A	45 A
Zn	044	098	156	207	267	290	335

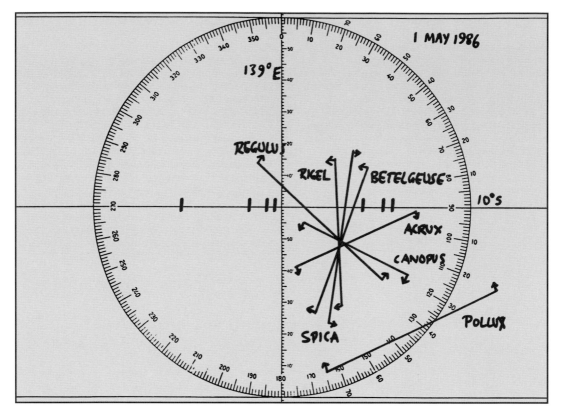

latitude will be the same for all the sights.

Here, then, is a worked example of a set of starsights.

Example

It is 1st May 1986. Your DR position is 10°S 139°E and evening twilight is approaching. What will be the time of civil twilight expressed in GMT at your position? Which stars will you go for? Your sextant has no index error.

From the daily pages of the almanac (see page 31) you'll see that civil twilight in 10°S is at 1811 on the Greenwich meridian.

139° = 9h 16 minutes and because civil twilight, like any other celestial event, will be earlier in east longitude, the GMT of civil twilight in 139°E will be 1811 — 916 = 0855 GMT.

You will not find the minutes and seconds for all the sights on the increments table given on page 16. Space forbids, I fear, so you'll have to take my word for it that the GHA increments are correct.

Don't forget that if you are in doubt as to whether to add or subtract the 9h 16 minutes, a quick look at your navigation clock will show

you the answer. You'll probably be doing the sum in mid-afternoon when the navigation clock shows about 0600 GMT and you know it's about three hours till twilight...

Once you've calculated the GMT time of civil twilight, enter it into the boxes on the upper part of the pro-forma and work out the LHA of Aries at your position for that time.

When you have the LHA you can enter Volume 1 of AP 3270. The illustration on page 39 shows a page for latitude 10°S. You can see the stars available and the Hc and Zn of each for the LHA you've worked out and for several others 'either side' of it.

The lower part of the pro-forma is filled out for the sights and times as they were actually taken. The plot illustrated shows the resulting position lines. Notice that there are no azimuths on the plot. With seven position lines to draw on the chart, marking in seven azimuths as well would just confuse the issue and make the plot unreadable. I generally lay my protractor up the direction of the azimuth from the AP, make a mark at the point where the intercept crosses it ('towards' or 'away', of course) and then construct the PL from that point by adding 90° to the direction of the azimuth.

Five of the position lines form a lovely fix, but you'll notice that Acrux is slightly outside, while Pollux is a long way adrift. In a situation like this it would be a safe assumption that what you thought was Pollux was something else (Castor, perhaps - this is not uncommon by any means). I would suggest discarding that one.

Acrux is not far out. There is a measurable possibility that it is right, so you might want to adjust your position accordingly. On the other hand you may recall having a struggle finding it. It was the first you took and it was very faint.

How good a sight was it? Only you can decide that one, but this is an example of the way you should evaluate your fix.

PRECESSION AND NUTATION

As the years roll on, the stars are creeping slowly to the westward across the celestial sphere. This movement is called *precession* and is generally considered at the same time as another tiny discrepancy to order, *nutation*, which is the name given to the amount that the Earth wobbles on its axis.

The combined effect of these two is that every ten years you need a new Volume 1 of AP 3270. If you have a '2000.0 Epoch' copy and it is 2004, look in the back and you will find a correction on Table 5. You should apply this (it is given in nautical miles and an angular direction) to your star fix to maintain its accuracy. It is also to be used on the PL from a single star being used for a fix against a planet, or some other body. It only concerns stars reduced through Volume 1.

10 Polaris
- the Pole Star

As every schoolboy knows, the Pole Star is located directly over the North Pole, for which it is named. Alone amongst the heavenly bodies it sits apparently still while the whole 'bowl of night' revolves in splendour around it.

Because of its unique situation dead on the Earth's axis, a corrected altitude of Polaris gives, without further ado, the observer's latitude. Long before the Sun's declination was tabulated, Polaris was giving heathen men a yardstick for north/south distance. They didn't know the Earth was round, so they had no idea why it worked. We do, and it works like this.

From the illustration you can see that since the terrestrial horizon is a tangent to the Earth's surface (and hence forms a right angle with the radius which designates the observer's latitude), the altitude of Polaris above this tangent is the same as the angle subtended by the observer's zenith at the centre of the Earth, that is, his latitude.

This works out because the distance to Polaris being effectively infinite, the line joining Polaris to the observer is parallel to the axis of the Earth.

CORRECTIONS TO THE APPARENT ALTITUDE OF POLARIS

Unfortunately, it seems that nothing in the universe is going to give us an even break. Even Polaris wanders from the pole by as much as two degrees. It is therefore necessary to apply some corrections to the apparent altitude (which as always is the sextant altitude corrected for index error and dip).

The first thing to do after correcting the sextant altitude to determine apparent altitude is to make the standard 'star' correction for refraction, as found in the middle column of the bookmark of the almanac (see page 35).

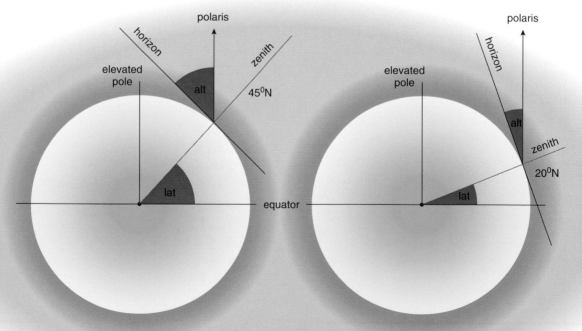

The altitude of Polaris (alt) is virtually the same as the observer's latitude (lat), regardless of whether the navigator is on a latitude of 45°N, as on the left, or 20°N, as on the right.

Having done this you enter the tables for Polaris immediately before the 'minutes and seconds' increment pages at the back of the almanac. There you will find three corrections: a_0, a_1, and a_2.

For a_0 you enter the tables with your LHA.

For a_1 you enter with your approximate latitude.

For a_2 you simply need to know what month it is.

The only work that you have to do here is solve the LHA of Aries for your approximate position at the time of your sight - to the nearest minute

of time is fine.

In order to keep the arithmetic simple, all the corrections are made positive, but when you have applied them all, you must subtract one degree from the final result to get your latitude. The pro-forma puts all this down in step-by-step form and should remove any doubts you may have about it.

Example

May 1st 1986. DR 51°N 20°W. Polaris is observed during morning twilight at 0552 GMT. Its sextant altitude is 51° 12´.6. Height of eye is 15 feet and index error is 2.8 *off* the arc. What is your latitude?

PRO FORMA FOR POLARIS

Date **1 MAY 1986**	Watch time	**05 52**
Approximate Latitude: **51°N**	Correction	**—**
DR Long **20° W**	GMT	**05 52**

GHA ♈ (hrs)	**293**	**50.0**
+ Increment (mins/secs)	**13**	**02**
GHA ♈	**306**	**52**
DR Long (approx)	**19**	**52**
LHA ♈	**287**	

Hs	**51**	**21.6**
Index error		**+2.8**
Dip		**-3.8**
Apparent Alt	**51**	**20.6**
Star Correction		**- 0.8**
Ho	**51**	**19.8**
+a_0 (LHA♈ **287°**)	**1**	**13.3**
+a_1 (Lat **51°N**)		**0.6**
+a_2 (month **MAY**)		**0.4**
Sum	**52**	**34.1**
-1°		**-1**
LATITUDE	**51° 34´.1 N**	

L.H.A. ARIES	240°–249°	250°–259°	260°–269°	270°–279°	280°–289°	290°–299°	300°–309°	310°–319°	320°–329°
	a_0	a_0	a_0	a_0	a_0	a_0	a_0	a_0	a_0
0	I 41·9	I 37·7	I 32·3	I 25·9	I 18·8	I 11·0	I 02·8	0 54·5	0 46·3
1	41·5	37·2	31·7	25·3	18·0	10·1	01·9	53·6	45·5
2	41·1	36·7	31·1	24·6	17·2	09·3	01·1	52·8	44·7
3	40·7	36·2	30·5	23·9	16·5	08·5	I 00·3	52·0	43·9
4	40·3	35·7	29·9	23·2	15·7	07·7	0 59·4	51·1	43·1
5	I 39·9	I 35·1	I 29·2	I 22·4	I 14·9	I 06·9	0 58·6	0 50·3	0 42·3
6	39·5	34·6	28·6	21·7	14·1	06·1	57·8	49·5	41·5
7	39·1	34·0	28·0	21·0	13·3	05·2	56·9	48·7	40·7
8	38·6	33·5	27·3	20·3	12·6	04·4	56·1	47·9	40·0
9	38·1	32·9	26·6	19·5	11·8	03·6	55·3	47·1	39·2
10	I 37·7	I 32·3	I 25·9	I 18·8	I 11·0	I 02·8	0 54·5	0 46·3	0 38·4
Lat.	a_1	a_1	a_1	a_1	a_1	a_1	a_1	a_1	a_1
0	0·5	0·4	0·4	0·3	0·2	0·2	0·2	0·2	0·3
10	·5	·5	·4	·3	·3	·3	·3	·3	·3
20	·5	·5	·4	·4	·4	·3	·3	·3	·4
30	·5	·5	·5	·4	·4	·4	·4	·4	·4
40	0·6	0·6	0·5	0·5	0·5	0·5	0·5	0·5	0·5
45	·6	·6	·6	·6	·5	·5	·5	·5	·5
50	·6	·6	·6	·6	·6	·6	·6	·6	·6
55	·6	·6	·6	·7	·7	·7	·7	·7	·7
60	·6	·7	·7	·7	·8	·8	·8	·8	·8
62	0·7	0·7	0·7	0·8	0·8	0·8	0·8	0·8	0·8
64	·7	·7	·8	·8	·9	·9	·9	·9	·8
66	·7	·7	·8	·9	0·9	0·9	0·9	0·9	0·9
68	0·7	0·8	0·9	0·9	I·0	I·0	I·0	I·0	I·0
Month	a_2	a_2	a_2	a_2	a_2	a_2	a_2	a_2	a_2
Jan.	0·5	0·5	0·5	0·5	0·5	0·5	0·6	0·6	0·6
Feb.	·4	·4	·4	·4	·4	·4	·4	·4	·5
Mar.	·4	·4	·3	·3	·3	·3	·3	·3	·3
Apr.	0·5	0·4	0·4	0·3	0·3	0·3	0·2	0·2	0·2
May	·6	·6	·5	·4	·4	·3	·3	·2	·2
June	·8	·7	·6	·6	·5	·4	·4	·3	·3
July	0·9	0·8	0·8	0·7	0·7	0·6	0·5	0·5	0·4
Aug.	·9	·9	·9	·8	·8	·8	·7	·6	·6
Sept.	·9	·9	·9	·9	·9	·9	·8	·8	·8
Oct.	0·8	0·8	0·9	0·9	0·9	0·9	0·9	0·9	0·9
Nov.	·6	·7	·8	·8	·9	·9	I·0	I·0	I·0
Dec.	0·5	0·5	0·6	0·7	0·8	0·8	0·9	I·0	I·0

Part of the tables for Polaris from the Nautical Almanac.
The ringed figures are those entered in the example pro-forma.

11 Compass checking on the ocean

When you are out on the ocean the only external means available for checking your compass are those provided by the sky.

It's always worthwhile to know that your deviation card is up-to-date when you are set up on a heading that may, wind permitting, stay more or less constant for days or even weeks. This is how it's done.

SUNSET AND SUNRISE: AMPLITUDE TABLES

Every proprietary nautical almanac should have a page devoted to tables known as amplitude tables. These give the bearing of the Sun in degrees True from your approximate position as it rises or sets.

LAT.	0°	1°	2°	3°	4°	DECLINATION 5°	6°	7°
	°	°	°	°	°	°	°	°
0° to 5°	90	89	88	87	86	85	84	83
6°	90	89	88	87	86	85	84	83
7°	90	89	88	87	86	85	84	83
8°	90	89	88	87	86	85	84	82.9
9°	90	89	88	87	86	85	83.9	82.9

A small section of the amplitude tables which give the bearing of the rising or setting Sun. You need to obtain the rough declination of the Sun from the daily pages of the almanac, and an approximate latitude.

If you are able to use your steering compass to take a bearing of the rising Sun, the difference between this and the bearing tabulated will be the total compass error. As you know, compass error is the sum of variation and deviation. Variation in a given area is known from the routeing charts used for ocean passage planning, so once you have applied that to a True bearing what is left can only be deviation.

It's worth noting that while pilot charts will last a lifetime in terms of wind and current, the variation curves they give do alter with the years. In the past, you either replaced them with new ones or turned to another source of up-to-date information on variation. The arrival of GPS receivers with course computers built in has removed this requirement. Most GPS sets will read out a 'course to steer' or 'course made good' in degrees true or degrees magnetic, corrected for zone and annual changes. Even if the read-out will not give the variation as a specific item, it is only necessary to program the instrument to give a course in magnetic, re-jig it to give the same one in true, then compare the two.

Points to note

Because of refraction, the Sun is technically 'rising' or 'setting' when it is one semidiameter

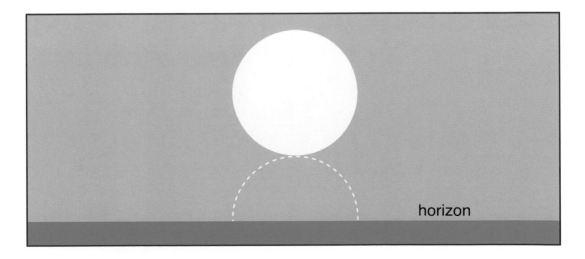

horizon

above the horizon, as in the illustration.

On east-west passages, the Sun often rises or sets on a bearing quite close to your course, either dead ahead or dead astern. If this is almost so, but not quite, a small course alteration to bring it right on the course line will give you its bearing from the steering compass. The difference in deviation between this heading and the course is unlikely to be significant.

If the Sun both sets and rises a large angular distance from your ship's heading then you'll have to measure its bearing relative to the ship's head. By applying that to the compass heading you can deduce its bearing on the steering compass.

The best way of taking the bearing of the setting or rising Sun is by sighting it directly across the steering compass. This is often possible where the instrument is mounted on a binnacle, or is the old-fashioned but ever-green Sestrel compass sited on the coachroof ahead of the cockpit. If you aren't lucky enough to have such an arrangement, you must take a bearing of the Sun relative to the ship's head by some mechanical means. The classic instrument for achieving such a bearing is a pelorus with proper sights and a finely graduated scale, but most yachts do not carry such a thing. However, nearly all use a chart plotter of some description. A workable relative bearing can be taken by setting this up somewhere on deck with zero degrees on the ship's head. You can use the moving arm of the plotter, if it has one, to sight on the Sun. Take some care to 'aim' the arm at the Sun's average position as the boat yaws from side to side of its course. You will have plenty of time to take pains and the results are usually quite satisfactory.

If sea conditions permit, I generally do this every time I'm able to observe the sunrise or the sunset. I enter the results in the back of my log book and maintain a running check on my ship's deviation card. This way any errors produced by using a chart plotter instead of a proper pelorus tend to average out, and any new errors are noticed straightaway.

Example:

Ship's Head by Steering Compass
250°C
Relative bearing of setting Sun
037°
∴ compass Bearing of sun
287°C
Bearing from amplitude tables
283°T
∴ total Compass Error
4°W

But, Variation (from pilot chart or GPS)
7°W
∴ deviation on this heading
3°East

AZIMUTHS FOR COMPASS CHECKS

Another excellent method of using the Sun to check your steering compass when your course is nowhere near the line of the rising or setting Sun is to wait until the Sun is dead ahead or dead astern, note its bearing, and take a sight.

It won't take a moment to work out just the azimuth part of the sight reduction calculation and once you have done so, you have your true ship's heading. You know your compass heading, the chart gives the local variation, so away you go...

12 The shortest way

We all know that the shortest distance from 'A' to 'B' is a straight line. Using a chart produced to the usual Mercator projection, a ruled line connecting two points will indicate a compass heading between them that does not vary. This 'rhumb line' course also represents more or less the least mileage where its length is insignificant compared with the size of the Earth. This feature of Mercator charts is eminently convenient for coastal work. At ocean scales, however, its practicality often breaks down.

Where a course line encompasses a substantial proportion of the globe, the inevitable distortions of the Mercator projection, particularly in higher latitudes, affect routeing to a serious degree.

GREAT CIRCLE SAILING

As we discussed on page 7 of this book, a great circle can be one of the meridians of longitude which converge at the poles but, apart from the equator, no parallel of latitude fits the description. A great circle, however, does not have to be one of these two. It is in fact any line depicted on the surface of the Earth by a plane which passes through its centre. The shortest distance between two points on the surface of a sphere is always the track of the great circle on which both are situated. When deciding which course to steer from one side of an ocean to the other, this is one of the factors you should consider.

Were you to sail a rhumb line on the Mercator projection of your chosen ocean, you will end up by travelling a more or less greater distance than you need have done, depending upon your latitude and how closely your course approaches due east or due west.

In high latitudes, on east-west headings, the rhumb line diverges substantially from the great circle route, while on similar headings on the equator (itself a great circle), they are one and the same. In any latitude a heading of due north or south is, by definition, a great circle, but as your headings swing away from this, the differences begin to compound.

In practice, if you are crossing the North Atlantic from Cape Race to the Bishop Rock and you are able to steer your desired course all the way, you will save several hundred miles by operating on the great circle. If you are crossing in the trades from the Cape Verdes to the Caribbean, any savings on the great circle track will be much smaller and will almost certainly be overshadowed by other considerations.

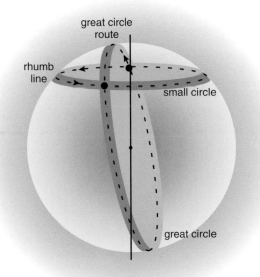

Right and above: On a Mercator chart a great circle route near the pole appears as a curved line, longer than the rhumb line. But if you look at the two routes as they appear on the globe, it is obvious that the great circle route is shorter.

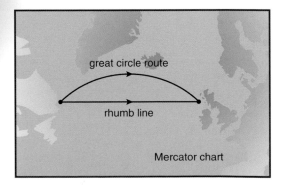

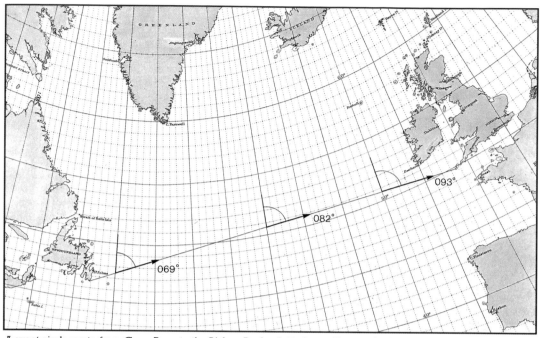

A great circle route from Cape Race to the Bishop Rock, plotted on a Gnomonic chart.

Working the Great Circle

Fortunately for the non-mathematical ocean navigator, charts covering all major routes are available upon which a straight line is, in fact, a great circle. This happy property of the Gnomonic projection makes planning a great circle route the simplest of tasks.

The illustration shows a Gnomonic chart of the North Atlantic, with the great circle route from Cape Race to the Bishop Rock drawn in. You will notice that it crosses each of the converging meridians at a slightly different angle. To determine the course at any particular meridian, you place your plotter north and south at the line of longitude and read off the course. Although ideally the course should change at each meridian, in practice you travel five or ten degrees and then lay off the next heading, proceeding in a series of rhumb lines from one great circle point to the next.

To lift a course from a Gnomonic chart you will need a plotter of the 'Breton' type or a small Douglas protractor. Parallel rules will be of little use. Lay the north-south line of the plotter grid along the charted meridian at your position, and read off the course from a light line plotted from it to the destination.

Navigators of steamers and motor yachts are advised to lift a series of points from their Gnomonic chart and pre-plot them onto a Mercator projection for day-to-day navigation

purposes. The results look like the diagram on page 62. This is not recommended for sailing craft because the nature of ocean weather generally dictates the detail of their tracks. As with navigation along the coast, it is rarely worth plotting a line along which you expect to travel, because however carefully you may plan a great-circle route, if you are in a sailing vessel I would stake a case of rum to a can of beer that you will not follow it.

A hundred miles out you will experience either a headwind or, in the trades, a wind that puts you onto a dead run. In neither case will you steer your course any more and all your planning will have been blown to bits.

What you actually do is this: Set out on a great circle with hope in your heart, but at all times sail your ship so as to travel as fast as sensibly possible in the most achievable comfort. Soon you'll be miles from your hoped-for track. Ocean navigation, like all navigation, consists of estimating or fixing your position and then shaping the best course you can from there to your destination. So after you have produced a decent fix and plotted it onto your Mercator chart, you then whip out your Gnomonic projection and pop it on there as well. Now lay off a new great circle heading. If you are lucky this one will last you more than a couple of days, but the sea and fore-and-aft rig being what they are, it probably won't.......

GPS and the Great Circle

An interesting development in great circle sailing which is a by-product of the GPS package is that the inbuilt course computer will automatically give you a course from your current position to your destination. All you have to do is punch in an arrival waypoint. At any time you need only press the 'go to' button and the computer will read out the distance and course to steer which, on most machines, will be a great circle. This theoretically renders the Gnomonic chart redundant but, for an old-fashioned chap like me, it's still reassuring to actually see the great circle laid out as a straight line across that weird grid.

COMPOSITE TRACKS

There can be any number of reasons why a pure great circle may take you to unacceptable places. Perhaps it skirts too closely unlit, isolated dangers. Maybe it goes too far towards the pole and the iceberg menace for your fancy, or perchance it is leading you into an area notorious for its lack of breeze. If any of these is the case, the usual solution is to follow the great-circle track until you arrive at the parallel of latitude which you have decided will delimit the danger, run east or west along it until the great circle re-emerges from the danger area and then join it once more to continue to your destination.

A classic example of this is a vessel running her easting down in the Southern Ocean with nearly half the globe to traverse. The great circle would pass far too close to the ice, so it is up to the skipper to decide by how much he wants to clear this hazard. When the chosen latitude is reached, course is altered to run as nearly as possible along the parallel. As soon as the great circle veers off towards the safe side of the danger zone, the yacht can re-join it.

Great circle sailing may only make a small difference in the Tropics, but the conscientious application of these principles as you sail the oceans in mid or high latitudes can save literally days. Every little helps when you are out there and, as Norie's definition of navigation points out, we must conduct our ships not only with 'the greatest safety' from one part of the ocean to another, but also 'in the shortest time possible'.

PRO-FORMA FOR SUN SIGHT

Date

Watch time
Correction
GMT

GHA (hrs)
+Correction (mins/secs)
GHA
Assumed Long
LHA

Assumed Lat

Hc   z   Declination (hrs)
d   180/360   d difference
Hc   Zn   Declination

Hs
Index Error
Dip
Apparent Alt
Main Correction
Ho
Hc
Intercept   TOWARDS/AWAY

A standard sunsight proforma. Together with shooting the Sun on your meridian for latitude, this is the most important sight you will take day by day. Understand this proforma and the others are simply a question of detail.

Part II: Deepwater meteorology

13　Ocean meteorology

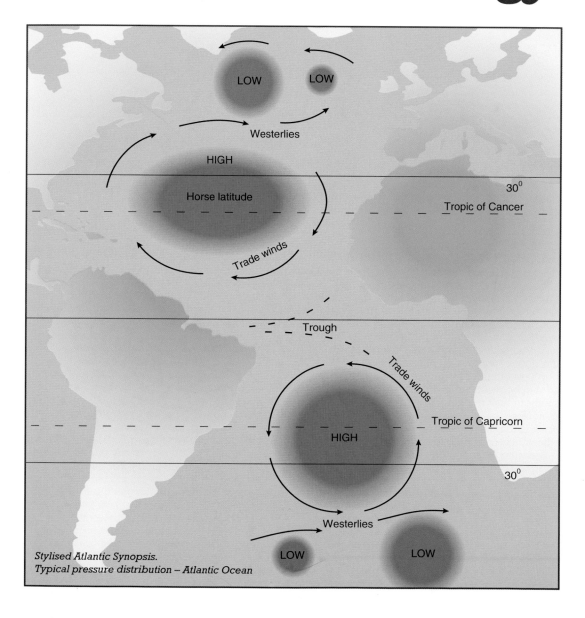

Stylised Atlantic Synopsis.
Typical pressure distribution – Atlantic Ocean

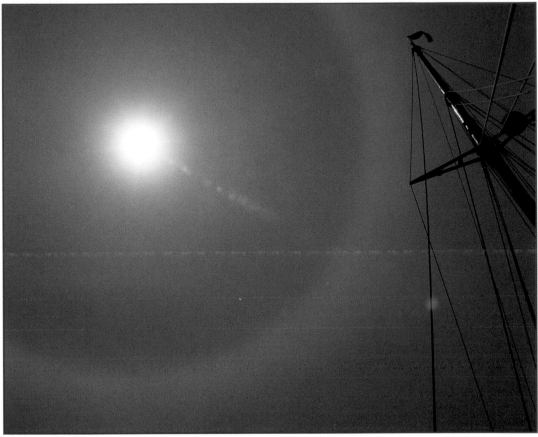

A halo of this magnitude round the Sun bodes no good.

The essential anatomy of mid-latitude wind systems will be well known to readers of this book. This stylised diagram of an Atlantic synoptic chart sums it up: in the northern half, a mid-oceanic high pressure system creates the right conditions for depressions in more northern latitudes to wind up a westerly airstream between about 40° and 55°. Along its southern limb the same high pressure circulation generates the northeast tradewinds, while in the slack isobars of its centre lie the Horse Latitudes where breeze is hard to come by.

A similar arrangement exists in the South Atlantic, with parallels in the North and South Pacific. It was in the North Atlantic, however, that the term 'Horse Latitude' was coined by explorers and conquistadors bound towards the New World with their full complement of beasts of war and burden. If their ships wandered from the trade routes into the airless centre of the high, they encountered Sargasso weed swirling aimlessly inside the system of currents that follow the ocean winds. As the ship's water

began to run out, they threw the horses overboard to conserve their own life supplies. These ill-fated mariners would have been well served by a pilot chart.

North of the depression centres in the northern hemisphere (or south of them in the southern) one does in theory encounter some easterly winds. These form the so-called 'Northern Route' across the North Atlantic, while far to the south, desperate square-rigger crews used to search for the easterlies, hacking ever towards Antarctica in a quest for a slant around the Horn. I can personally testify that the year I crossed the North Atlantic westbound via Iceland and Southern Greenland these following winds were a figment of the met books' propaganda. We beat more or less the whole way. Perhaps others have had better luck. Knowledge of this general circulation will be of use in planning a passage and it is worth noting that, on the whole, ocean currents follow the same pattern as the winds, drifting before the prevailing airstream.

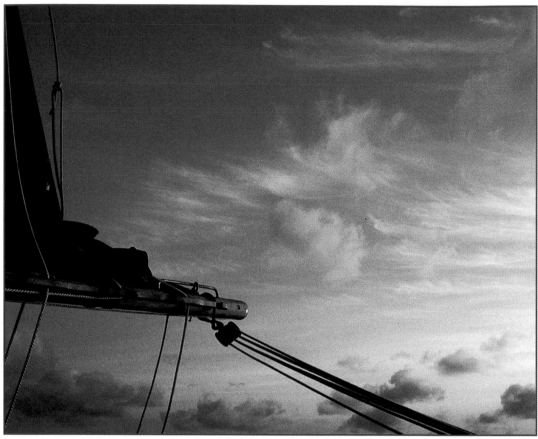

Cirrus cloud streaming across from the west, with Cirrostratus on its heels, suggests a warm front is on its way.

Practical mid-latitude weather and forecasting it

Outside the tropics, ocean weather behaves more or less as sailors are used to it on the continental shelf. There are, however, two striking features.

First, because there is no running away from it, you will generally experience more heavy weather on ocean trips than you ever have in coastal waters. Some of the details of surviving storms at sea are dealt with in *Heavy Weather Cruising* (Fernhurst Books), but the major tactical effect is that there are no harbours to escape to and no snug berths to hide in while the gale blows itself out. It is therefore axiomatic that your boat is properly found to cope with heavy weather. Waves will usually be bigger than you are used to, but on the positive side, there are no rocks and no lee shores. Except *in extremis*, therefore, you are probably safer out there than nearer home, though there will be times when it may not feel that way.

The second thing you will notice about weather at sea in the 'forties and fifties' is that depressions behave far more like the book says they will than is often the case near land. Without large lumps of solid stuff to distort their purity, they tend to appear on synoptic charts as they are depicted in text books. The results are dramatic.

Fronts associated with ocean depressions are normally obvious. Cold fronts can be particularly lively, with winds clocking sharply toward the pole and a change in precipitation which you cannot miss. Unpleasant though this may be, it is comforting to know that before long life will improve – for a while at least.

In fair weather, the warm front that heralds a depression can usually be seen approaching for some time. First comes a fine array of high cirrus cloud spreading over the western sky. Maybe it is accompanied by a halo round the sun or moon. You could ignore these portents, but in my experience this can be unwise. Next, the barometer begins to tumble while the wind

shifts and hardens.

If the glass is falling at one millibar in three hours, you can be reasonably sure that something unpleasant is on the way. Two millibars per three hours normally heralds gale-force winds, especially if the rate of fall continues for eight hours or more, while if the dial collapses by five millibars in three hours you know you're for it, with storm-force winds shortly to become your portion. When it's going to blow, a swell coming from the upwind direction will be noticeable.

These signals are so unmistakable in deep water that they are usually all a sailor in a small boat needs. The use of more modern methods to keep out of trouble will be considered later, but the truth is that in medium and high latitudes you will probably get most of what's coming unless you have a very fast boat. At least, this kind of 'single station forecasting' prepares you for the worst. It may be reassuring to hear a voice on a long-range radio tell you it's only going to blow force seven, or peer at the wind arrows on an Internet download, but out there at the coal face it's reality that counts.

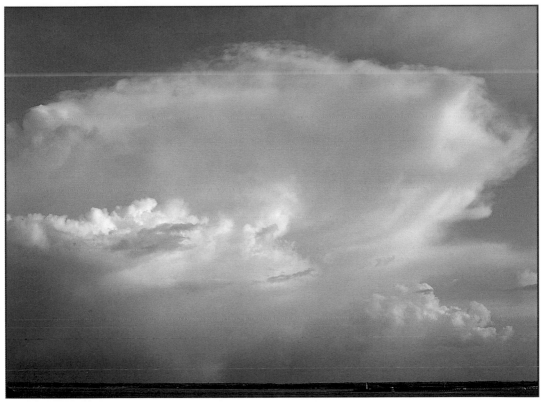

Classic cumulonimbus. A veering wind and rising glass are a sure indication of the passage of a cold front. Expect an improvement in the weather - for a while at least.

14 Tropical weather

Contrary to what one might imagine after reading the travel brochures, many tropical areas do not enjoy a year-round idyllic climate. A typical example is the situation in the Windward and Leeward Islands of the West Indies. This sometimes ideal cruising ground sits plumb in the tropical belt of the western North Atlantic. From early winter through until early summer, the area has more or less reliable tradewind weather of the sort many of us leave home to find. In high summer, however, the cool, steady breeze gives way to hot, airless days. For all but the southernmost islands, there develops the permanent threat of a major beating from a hurricane.

Similar scenarios exist in many tropical locations. As a result, it is as important to make sure that you are in the right place at the right time in low latitudes as it is in high. The consequences of being too casual may sometimes be less obvious, but they could be dire indeed.

Tradewind sailing

As the winds blow around the equatorial quadrants of the mid-ocean 'highs' they settle into the constant tradewinds. The steady easterlies follow the track of the isobars, but since these tend to 'flatten out' opposite the equator, the winds often stay consistent in direction for hundreds, even thousands, of miles. According to accepted theory, the trades bring fair weather and blow at a mean speed of around 14 knots — a pretty picture indeed.

Unfortunately, reality is often different from the sailor's dreams. Reading cruising classics from the 1950s, one might be forgiven for believing the tradewinds to be as reliable as sunrise, but it does seem that nowadays they are less predictable, with yachts reporting crossings of light and variable conditions where there should have been a steady following breeze.

Sometimes, the trades can blow great guns. In the West Indies, for example, the so-called 'Christmas Winds' are exceedingly stiff. I can recall spending one festive season anchored in the lee of St Kitts with so much breeze that it was impossible to row ashore in a fine stem dinghy to replenish the necessities of celebration. We sailed for eight weeks that winter with two reefs and a spitfire jib on a thirtyfive-ton cutter, and we were not under-canvassed.

Squalls

Watch out for squalls in the tradewinds. There are sometimes more of them than you might imagine and they can raise the wind speed substantially. If you cannot see the horizon underneath a cloud, expect rain for sure and probably a blow lasting anything from five to twenty minutes.

If you are reaching or beating, squalls can be handled by bearing away to reduce the apparent wind and the heeling effect. The blow may last a little longer than if you press on regardless, and you may be giving away a mile or two of weather gauge, but at the time it will seem cheap at the price. Soon it will pass; with luck the wind will return to normal, the Sun will re-emerge and you can get back to watching the flying fish play.

Working across the trades

When considering a route that involves reaching across the tradewind, or one which would place you as close to the wind as you can comfortably lie, most cruisers will end up steering at least 60° off the true wind. You may even plump for more. There is generally an eight-foot sea running in these latitudes and you won't enjoy pointing up any higher unless you happen to be racing. It will all even out in the end, however. It's better to arrive with the teeth still in your head and the mast in your boat than to hammer yourself to pieces trying to fight the unconquerable.

If you are considering a trip that may involve beating a serious distance against the tradewind, there is only one answer. Don't, if you can possibly go somewhere else. There is usually a current running down the trades; tacking against it can be like trying to weather a major headland against a foul tide that will never turn.

The Intertropical Convergence Zone

This is a trough of low pressure which extends across the oceans between the influences of the

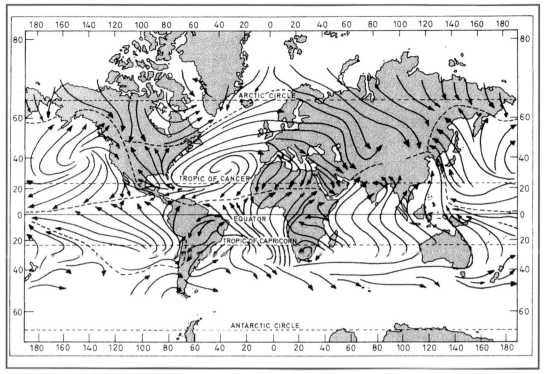

Mean surface winds in July. (Extracted from Reed's excellent Maritime Meteorolgy *by Cornish & Ives.)*

north and south high pressure systems. It represents the convergence of air from the two hemispheres and, while not technically a weather front, it does display some front-like characteristics when you are sailing through it. Known as the ITCZ, this band of recognisable weather stretches across the Atlantic and Pacific Oceans all the year round. In the Indian Ocean it is sucked north onto the continent of Asia during the Southwest Monsoon and is of no interest to the sailor.

The ITCZ is generally at its widest on the eastern sides of the oceans, where the widespread calm, or rainy and squally conditions are known as 'doldrums'. Further westwards, the northeast and southeast trades come ever closer together, sometimes merging into a general easterly as the ocean's western extremity is approached.

Sailing across the ITCZ can be almost unnoticeable or it can be decidedly unpleasant. Sometimes the calms mentioned above are a real problem, at other times they seem barely to exist, being substituted by days of grey, rainy weather punctuated by nasty squalls. In the Atlantic, a south-bound skipper's dilemma is typically that the further west the yacht crosses the line, the less trouble she will have from the

ITCZ, but the more close-hauled she will be when she picks up the southeast trades and has to weather the corner of Brazil. Life is rarely perfect for the ocean sailor.

Monsoons

Just as temperature variations of land and sea on a summer's afternoon cause pressure differences resulting in sea breezes, far mightier results occur on a global scale from similar causes. In the summer months, pressure generally falls as continental land masses cook up. It remains comparatively high over the oceans. The reverse effect occurs in winter. In some areas the outcome of these phenomena is a predictable, reversing wind circulation known as a 'monsoon'.

The Indian Ocean, The South China Sea and Northern Australia

The effects of low pressure over northwest India from May through September are felt right down into the southern hemisphere. The pressure gradient stretches into the southeast trades of the Indian Ocean, which are drawn northwards to cross the equator, veering southwesterly as they become part of the monsoon circulation.

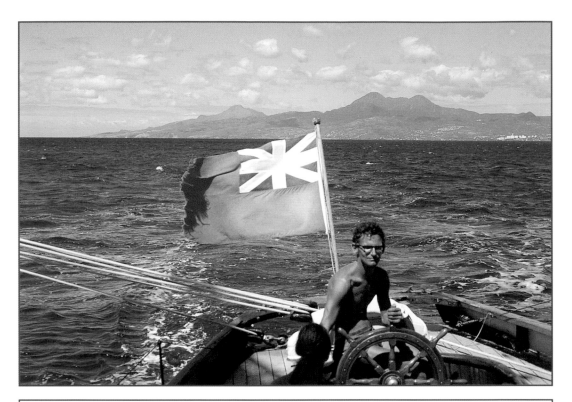

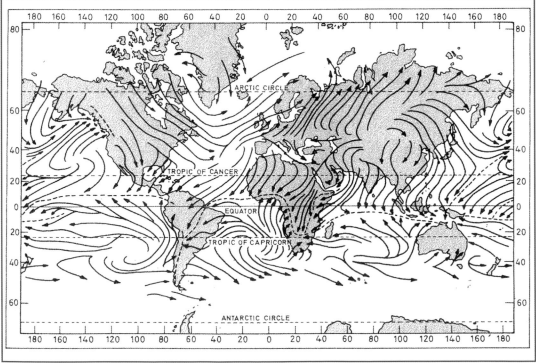

Mean surface winds in January. (Extracted from Reed's excellent Maritime Meteorolgy *by Cornish & Ives.)*

Any northeast trades in the northern Indian Ocean and as far away as the western part of the North Pacific are knocked out completely and replaced by the monsoon sou'wester.

This southwest monsoon is an extremely wet wind in the Bay of Bengal and it blows hard. In the China Sea, it is less violent and considerably drier. Here, its flow is often east of south, but despite its comparatively well-mannered appearance, it can still generate typhoons right into October. Cyclones in the Indian Ocean are also prevalent towards the end of the period.

From October to March, the Indian Ocean comes under the influence of a huge high over Siberia. This funnels a more pleasant northerly airstream over the area which starts northeasterly, gradually backs northwest as it crosses the equator and reaches Australia under the name of the 'Northwest Monsoon'

In the northern half of the Indian Ocean, this monsoon is dry and usually brings fair weather. Further away along the China and Indochina coasts, winds are stronger. Between January and April, particularly later in the period, overcast weather with prevalent drizzle known as 'Crachin' occurs over the South China Sea.

Other Monsoons

In West Africa, a southwest monsoon blows into the Gulf of Guinea from around June to September. Its effects can stretch to 20° South. Low pressure over the Amazon Basin causes a northeast monsoon tendency down the eastern coast of Brazil from September to March. There are also frequently-disguised monsoon cycles in other areas, including the Gulf of Mexico.

The Tropical Revolving Storm
By far the most dreaded horror the tropic seas have in store for the sailor is the Tropical Revolving Storm, or 'TRS' as it is known. These storms, their avoidance and management are dealt with in chapters 15 and 16.

15   The Tropical Revolving Storm

The tropical revolving storm (TRS) is the planet's most violent weather system. Under their various guises of hurricane (North Atlantic), typhoon (China Seas) or cylcone (Indian Ocean), these cyclonic disturbances cause more mayhem every year than most commentators would care to quantify. In 1970, a cyclone rampaged ashore on the Bay of Bengal, killing half a million people and unleashing energy that has been likened to the same number of atomic bombs.

It is not only the Third World that suffers from these terrible storms. In 1992, Hurricane *Andrew* left upwards of a quarter million homeless in Florida and ran up an unsettled account for 25 billion dollars. What happens to a yacht at sea in such conditions is effectively indescribable. To make certain that it does not happen to you, it is first necessary to understand the nature of the beast. In Chapter 16, we will consider what tactics can best be adopted if you should ever find yourself sighting up the wrong end of this grizzly proposition. First, we shall study its anatomy.

Early life and nature of a TRS

Most TRS activity originates from shallow tropical wave depressions running down the tradewind, or major cloud disturbances associated with the Intertropical Convergence Zone. They require a limitless supply of warm, moist air, for which the critical criterion is a sea temperature of around 80 °F (26 °C) — only generally achieved in tropical seas during late summer and autumn. This proposition holds good even in the Indian Ocean and Arabian Sea where, although a TRS can occur at either change of monsoon, they are at their worst in the usual northern hemisphere danger-months of July to October. These storms cannot form within 5° of the equator because in this area there is not enough coriolis 'spin' to wind up the circulation.

As moist air rises over the warm sea, an area of low pressure is formed which may develop a circulatory motion if it becomes enough of a feature for the coriolis force of the turning Earth to grab hold of it. Once this occurs it is designated a 'tropical depression', defined by winds of Force 7 or less, but it now has the potential to wind up into something far worse. The rising air in the centre of such a system gives off latent heat as its moisture precipitates out at higher altitudes. This keeps it rising until it runs out of moisture at anything up to eight miles high. The newly dried air is spun out at the top of the depression as it begins to circulate with real power. The air now travels to the outer limits of influence of the centre, where it is sucked down

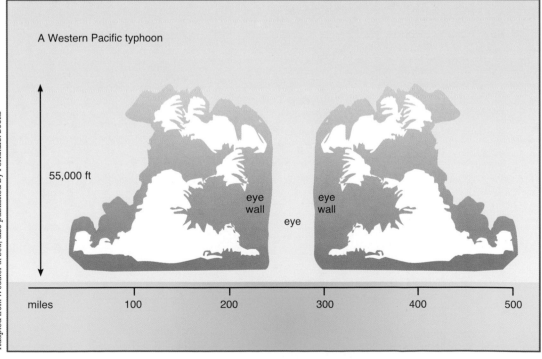

A Western Pacific typhoon

55,000 ft

eye wall

eye wall

eye

miles   100   200   300   400   500

Adapted from *Weather at Sea*, also published by Fernhurst Books

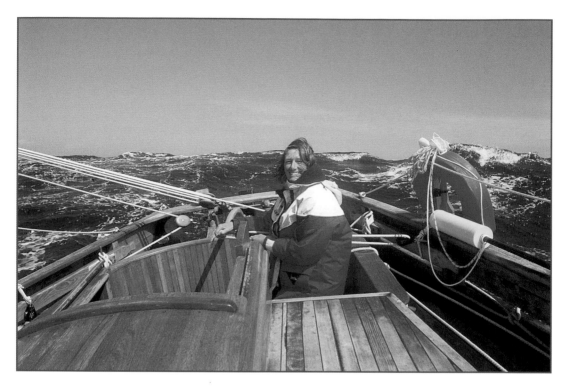

towards sea level again. Close to the water once more, it loads up on moisture, spirals inwards towards the centre and repeats its journey at ever-more frenetic velocity.

As the huge 'heat engine' cranks itself up, winds near what is now the eye increase to anything from 35 to 55 knots and before long Force 12 is reached. This is 60 knots and a full hurricane, cyclone or typhoon is born.

The storm can be anything from 50 to something approaching 1,000 miles in diameter, although typical sizes range between 150 and 250 miles. Wind speeds may rise into the realms of the unimaginable. Hurricane *Gilbert* wound up to 139 knots in 1988, *Luis* managed 120 knots in September 1995 and rampaged through the Caribbean with terrible results for St Martin and Antigua. 180 knots have been mentioned, but a more typical wind speed, for Atlantic hurricanes at any rate, is around 90 knots.

Life in the storm's eye, or 'vortex', is remarkable for the fact that an observer may well have clear blue sky overhead, while towering up on all sides are the mighty clouds of the eye 'wall'. Rainfall in the circulatory system will have been phenomenal, and seas will have built to enormous proportions. Once in the eye, rain stops while the seas, temporarily bereft of the wind that was giving them some discipline, become totally confused and mountainous. As

the eye passes, the wind returns from a different direction, the rain begins once more and the seas slowly sort themselves out, although this is purely relative.

The mid-life, routes and death of a TRS

A TRS normally grows as it travels. Its pressure may not sound staggeringly low to a sailor from higher latitudes used to winter depressions of 950 millibars. A TRS may only run to 960 millibars, although far lower readings, such the exceptional central pressure of 888 millibars achieved by *Gilbert,* have been recorded. What is extraordinary is the pressure gradient, which can be as much as 10 millibars over 50 miles with even greater falls towards the centre.

It is impossible to be specific about the movements of a typical TRS, but it can be said with only rare contradiction that most Atlantic and Pacific examples begin their lives south of their mid-oceanic subtropical 'high', sometimes a good way east. They then travel west or northwest (southwest in the southern hemisphere), slowly at first, before accelerating to 10 or 12 knots as they approach the twentieth parallel. Somewhere around here, many northern storms 'recurve' in a clockwise direction (anti-clockwise in the south) and move at increasing velocity away from the tropics.

This may also carry them further from the land mass on the west side of the ocean. The centre of recurvature of a storm is called the 'vertex' of its track – not to be confused with the 'vortex'.

In the most general terms, a recurving TRS will follow the isobars of the mid-latitude anticyclone, or 'high', but even with modern computer models and all the other wonders of science, TRS tracks remain notoriously unpredictable. Occasionally a storm will perform a full loop, which forecasters may at first assume to be the recurving process.

As a TRS travels towards temperate latitudes after recurving, its size increases and ultimately it loses its tropical identity by developing into a frontal depression or becoming absorbed into the circulation of a temperate system that has already formed.

The alternative scenario is that the recurving procedure does not take place and the storm goes barrelling ashore with catastrophic results. It is not unusual for this to happen when a North Atlantic hurricane piles into Florida, or enters the Gulf of Mexico after marching down the Greater Antilles chain. It then turns right and pulverises the Deep South of the US. Another area where recurvature tends to fail is the Bay of Bengal, leaving the low-lying Ganges delta a helpless victim.

When a tropical storm comes ashore, its days are numbered and it is doomed literally to 'run out of steam' from lack of water, the fuel of its engine. Occasionally, however, they have enough inherent energy to leap-frog the land and reappear back at sea to wind themselves up again. This can occur in Central America, while cyclones have been known to travel clear across India to re-establish themselves in the Arabian Sea.

16 Navigating in the vicinity of a Tropical Revolving Storm

Strategic TRS avoidance

The primary factor in TRS avoidance is a question of strategy. Be somewhere else. Because of the unpredictability of tropical cyclones, one can never be absolutely sure of missing them by working the seasons, but you can easily whittle down your chance of being hit, from a fair possibility to the almost negligible. Nobody is going to put his hand on his heart and say, 'If you cross the Atlantic from the Canaries to the Caribbean at Christmas, you are guaranteed not to see a hurricane', but those of us who have made such trips in winter have not spent our time nervously scanning the sky and tuning our PCs in to the hurricane advisory service. The likelihood is extremely slim. Find out what your local TRS season is going to be, then plan accordingly.

Sometimes, it may be necessary to be out on the ocean at times when TRS activity is a measurable possibility. An example would be a decision to sail to Bermuda from the US in late October. You might do this in order to miss the beginning of the New England winter, before moving south to the Caribbean a few weeks later when the hurricane season is virtually closed. Hurricanes can form in October and do recurve towards Bermuda. All in all, however, the chance might be considered worth taking, especially with a clear forecast to start the trip. The bottom line is that unless you plot your whole cruising curriculum with TRS avoidance as the sole item on the agenda you must accept the possibility, however remote, that you may one day be hit.

So what are the signs that a tropical storm is coming your way?

Warnings from your own observations

Barometer

The first tell-tale is your barometer, just as it is in more temperate latitudes. In the tropics, the barometer is generally rock steady for days on end, except for the phenomenon of 'diurnal variation'. Typically, this involves a rhythmic pulsing of pressure of between 1 and 1.6 millibars on either side of the normal. The cycle happens twice a day, with 'highs' around 1000 and 2200 local time, and lows corresponding at 0400 and 1600. Mean pressure comes an hour or so after noon and midnight.

You soon get used to diurnal variation when sailing the tropics. If you see the pressure nudge up a notch, watch out. This might indicate a TRS between 500 and 1,000 miles off. When it starts to drop, note readings regularly. A drop of three millibars or more means you should take matters seriously. A five millibar drop means that you could well be within 200 miles of a TRS.

Swell

It will come as no surprise to learn that a TRS shoves a mighty sea in front of it as it moves. A high swell with a rapid period is often the first sign because these seas can extend up to a thousand miles ahead of the system. They travel faster than the storm, so you may become aware of them a day or more before the barometer starts its tricks.

Don't assume that the eye of a TRS is advancing at ninety degrees to the wave pattern. It may be, but as we shall see, the outer winds do not run directly along the isobars. In any event, unless you have other information, the storm could well have changed course since

it kicked up the waves that are passing you at any particular moment.

Sky

Visibility sometimes becomes crystal clear during the approach of a TRS. Evening and morning skies may be vividly coloured as cirrus cloud develops, sometimes in a series of 'vees' pointing towards the distant eye. Cirrus is seen from 300 to 600 miles from the vortex and, together with the swell, may be the first indication that all is going to be far from well. As the storm approaches, the cloud levels lower with altostratus and fractocumulus giving way to driving, rain-soaked black scud.

Wind

Because there are no fronts in a TRS, the airstream runs directly around it. Winds spiral anti-clockwise in the northern hemisphere and clockwise in the southern. In the outer regions there is considerable in-draught across the isobars — up to 45° at 200 miles from the centre, where the wind will typically be blowing Force 6 or 7. As the eye-wall is approached, the winds rattle straight round the circle, the centrifugal force virtually defeating the pressure difference.

In the absence of any radio forecasting, this information is critical for locating the storm centre as it approaches. At first, therefore, if you face the wind, the eye of the storm will be around 120° on your right (left in the southern hemisphere). As things hot up, the angle will decrease until the vortex is at hand, at which point its middle should be square to your shoulder.

Tactical avoidance and storm management

With a TRS moving at fifteen knots or so, the idea of the average cruising yacht outrunning one is rarely realistic. It can, however, be possible to side-step its worst effects.

First, the storm's relative position and track should be ascertained as closely as possible by applying the above principles coupled, where possible, with weather reports (see Chapter 17). Now comes the big decision about tactics. The best action will depend upon which 'quadrant' of the approaching TRS you seem to be in. For clarity, we will consider a northern hemisphere TRS, but note the opposite wind directions, etc. for the southern hemisphere

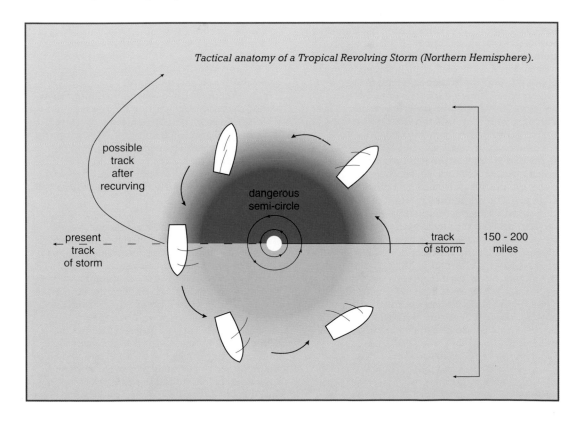

Tactical anatomy of a Tropical Revolving Storm (Northern Hemisphere).

possible track after recurving

dangerous semi-circle

present track of storm

track of storm

150 - 200 miles

shown in the illustration.

The dangerous semicircle

This is the semicircle on the storm's 'starboard side' as it advances. Because of the anticlockwise circulation of air and the forward motion of the storm which creates its own apparent wind, the wind across the deck of a stationary vessel on this side can be 20 to 30 knots greater than that on the opposite side, where the speed of the system's progress is effectively subtractive. Furthermore, because it is to this side that the storm will recurve (if it has not already done so), a boat caught in its dangerous sector may be in for a 'double whammy' if her luck is out.

A yacht trying to evade the eye from a position within the dangerous sector would have to attempt to sail close-hauled or pretty near to it, as fast and as far as possible. Anyone who has tried this in 40 knots of true wind (45 knots on the anemometer) in open water will understand that even to contemplate it in 60 knots plus is a non-starter for a cruising yacht. Therefore, if it seems that an approaching storm will catch you in the forward quadrant of this semicircle, you need a quick decision. Either you must beat as far beyond the track of the centre as you can while you still may, taking your chance on a recurvature hit, or you should put the wind on the starboard quarter and run as fast as you can, trying to reach the slightly less awesome 'navigable' semicircle.

A further problem associated with the dangerous semicircle, or at least its forward quadrant, is that a yacht caught in it and not making way will be carried into the track of the eye. So, if you find yourself in this most wretched of circumstances without the option of running out of it, you have little choice but to make what ground you can by sailing or motorsailing with serious dedication on starboard. When either you or the boat can stand it no more, you must heave to on that tack if you can still carry any rags of canvas, batten down, and put your trust in fate, your god, or whoever rigged your boat.

Even when you are 'abaft the beam' of the storm's eye, your problems are not over in the dangerous semicircle. You are now in its aft quadrant, but still the wind is driving you towards the centre. Your only comfort is that so long as it doesn't recurve on top of you, the TRS is on its way to bother somebody else.
The nature of the dangerous semicircle is so uncompromising that if it seems likely to become your lot in an approaching storm, you simply must take positive and early action either to avoid it on the right of the storm's path, or muscle your way across to its left into the navigable semicircle before it is too late. With a reasonable warning of the storm's approach, the latter may prove a possibility, in which case you are far from helpless.

If a TRS is advancing at 10 knots and it is three or four hundred miles away, you may have manageable winds for another fifteen hours, possibly longer. Most modern cruisers can achieve 100 miles in that time. If the storm was going to catch you 50 miles from the centre inside its dangerous semicircle, a determined effort across its approach line would place you the same distance on the safer side. What is more, since most boats can run in far heavier going than they can beat into, you will still be able to sail towards clearer conditions long after you'd have had to heave to in the dangerous quadrant. Plus, a storm will rarely alter course towards the equator, whither you will initially be bound. It might even do you a favour and recurve before it reaches you, making your action still more successful.

The navigable semicircle

Life in this half of the TRS will still be hell, but your chances of a safe exit are greater than the poor chaps we have just been discussing. You also have a better probability of being able to side-step the worst of the action as it approaches. The danger of a cruelly-timed recurvature is almost (though never totally) non-existent, and in order to increase your distance from the track of the approaching centre, you can reach bravely with the wind exactly where you want it, broad on the quarter.

There is thus only one tactic on this side of the storm and its approaches: crack on while you can. The skipper who has been hesitant will surely take a worse pasting than the one who 'went for it' when he could. Even if you end up running under bare poles, the more ground you can make, the safer you will be. This is because when the storm centre is 'abeam' and your course appears 'inwards' of parallel to its track, it is continuing to move onwards, away from you as you run.

Should you find yourself unable to carry on and you are sailing a boat that can lie a'hull without committing suicide (and some can), the wind is still blowing you past the moving vortex.

The final word is, don't give up and lie down. Never stop thinking, maintain a well-found ship with a bullet-proof self-steering system, and keep your courage up. You'll probably pull through with tales to tell for a lifetime.

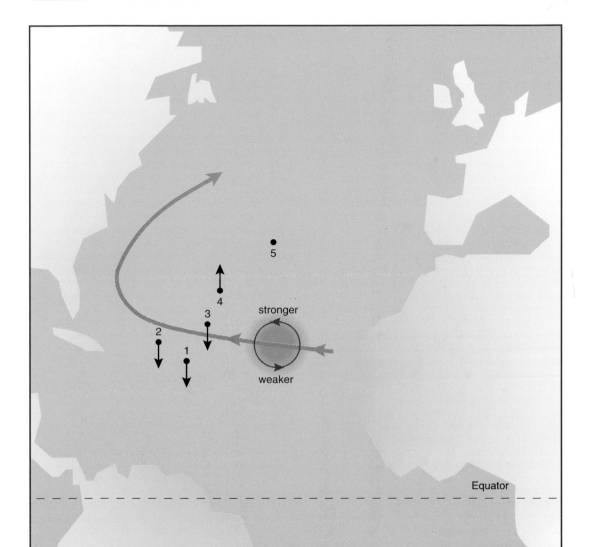

Handling an approaching Tropical Revolving Storm in the northern hemisphere.

1,2 Get south of the track of the storm,
i.e. towards the equator.
3   Probably best to run south of the likely storm
track, depending on the nature
of the storm, speed of approach etc.
4   Move north or northeast,
i.e. at right angles to the storm track.
5   Wait. Be ready if it recurves.

17 Modern weather forecasting and communications

Radio Weather Forecasts

By Voice
It isn't so long since the only weather reports of use to ocean mariners came in Morse Code down short-wave sets, usually driven by professional radio operators. Today, not only can yachts receive comprehensive weather information by voice, there are even inter-active stations where the sailor can discuss his situation with experts ashore.

It is important that you do your 'homework' on weather stations before you leave, because availability varies from ocean to ocean and depends entirely on what equipment you have.

The essential reference work is the *Admiralty List of Radio Signals, Volume III, Radio Weather Services*. This gives you the word on official marine weather broadcasts via HF (SSB), VHF, Weatherfax and Navtex. In addition to this government information, many voyage routes are covered by Ham nets and private individuals whose lives are dedicated to assisting sailors. Some have user-friendly names, like 'Trudy's

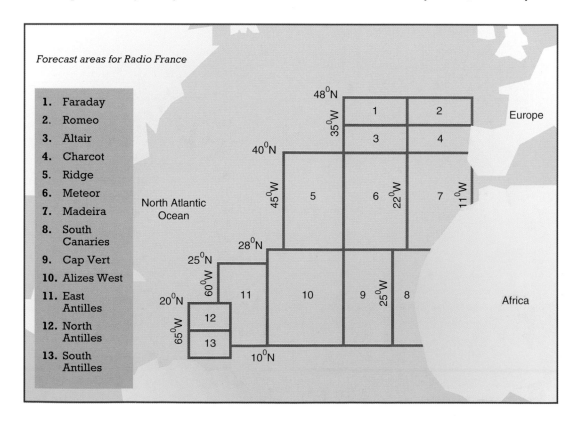

Forecast areas for Radio France

1. Faraday
2. Romeo
3. Altair
4. Charcot
5. Ridge
6. Meteor
7. Madeira
8. South Canaries
9. Cap Vert
10. Alizes West
11. East Antilles
12. North Antilles
13. South Antilles

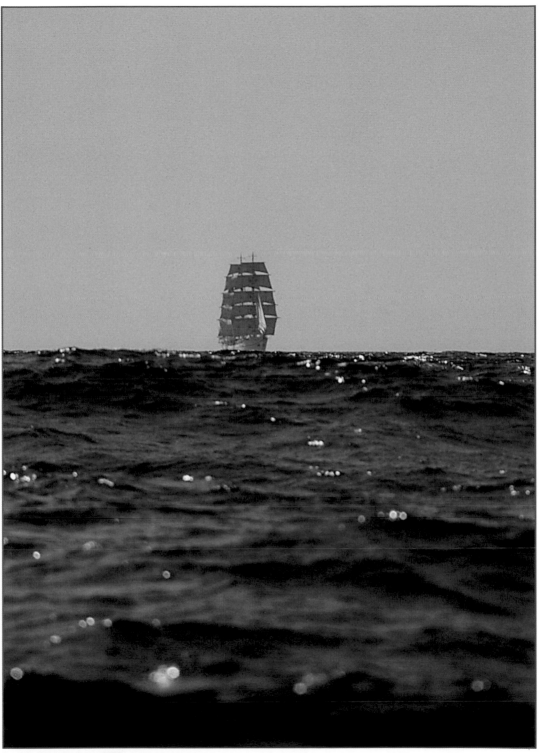

In the days before GPS...

Maritime Mobile Ham Net' which deals with the North Atlantic and Caribbean and is on the air at around 1300 UTC on 21.400 Mhz.

A useful North Atlantic station is 'Herb' Hilgenberg in Canada. Herb is good value even if you don't have a transmitter, because listening to his recommendations for other yachts that do have one can flesh out an otherwise thin appreciation of the overall situation. Herb is on callsign VAX498 on 12.359 Mhz at 2000 UTC. Another such ham is Bill Hall (callsign G4FRN) who runs the UK Maritime Mobile Net talking to yachtsmen world-wide. Bill listens to weather information, relays it and occasionally takes action to initiate rescue procedures if he hears of an emergency. He comes on the air at 0800 UTC on 14.303 Mhz, while his co-operator, Bruce (G4Y2H) covers an evening session.

Official information on weather system centres and their movements in the western North Atlantic comes from 'Perfect Paul', or 'Iron Mickey' as some know him. This is a robot voice put out four times daily by the US Coast Guard (NMN).

Similar nets are available in the Pacific, e.g. South Pacific Cruising Net at 7.076 MHz at 1800 UTC, the Mediterranean with Maritime Net Greece/Turkey (12.353 at 0645 UTC) and others. Languages other than English are also catered for and the French 'Radio France International' at 1130 UTC is probably the best forecast for crossing the trades to the Caribbean from Europe. If you have high-school French and you listen regularly, you'll start to decipher it quite quickly using the map illustrated.

All these stations are available on a good quality pocket-sized short-wave receiver, available in your local radio store for around £200. You may not even need to rig an outside aerial. The Sony package comes complete with a suitable length of reeled-up wire and a connector to hook it up to the usual telescopic aerial you would find on any portable VHF receiver. I have draped mine around the deckhead of my navigation station and picked up Perfect Paul, Herb and others satisfactorily. It doesn't stop the gales coming, but at least I know what to expect.

Weather via fax, satellite and the Internet

Weatherfax information is now readily available to yachts, giving current synoptic charts as well as prognoses. Already, however, yachts who want to remain in touch with the world ashore will be able to hook up via satellite to the telephone network and hence to the Internet through their on-board PC.

Weather services available on the Internet are many even now and seem sure to proliferate in the future. Various providers offer synoptic charts free of charge. By comparing these, together with the accompanying comments and data, a sailor can form conclusions about which outfit is currently to be preferred. For those who want to spend the money, tailor-made forecasts can be issued to you personally by a number of providers.

Detailed Internet information on TRS development is astonishing. Hurricanes in the North Atlantic can be followed by courtesy of at least five different providers. All deliver coloured maps, histories of current storms, forecasts and numerical data. Sea ice data proliferation is not far behind. Armed with such information, a yacht has a better chance than ever before of staying clear of trouble.

Only a quarter century ago, the vast majority of ocean cruising yachts were 'single station forecasters'. They left port with what information they could gather and put out with only a barometer, the sea and the sky as their guides. There will always be sailors who prefer their voyaging like that and choose to keep it so. For the mainstream, however, the future lies in a 'laptop' hooked up to the world, interfaced with GPS and an electronic chart plotting program. No longer will most of us sail free under the heavens, content to make the best of what comes and with only a general idea of our where-abouts. Instead, we will watch our yachts crawl across a screen, our position defined to within a boat's length. Wanted and unwanted e-mail messages will flow from our PCs and an accurate, up-to-date weather chart will be overlaid onto the ocean we are sailing. It's progress. Some will choose to reject the changes, but growing numbers would feel uneasy without them, for we live increasingly in an age of certainties.

Part III: The Ocean Passage

18 Ocean Passage Planning

Any sailor with enough experience to set out across his first ocean will be aware of the importance of passage planning. For the coastal navigator, a bad plan or no plan at all can result in a trip that could have taken five pleasant hours turning into a ten-hour epic of misery. Such woe would result from a skipper failing to consider crucial tidal information, or ignoring a weather forecast for 'head winds today, fair breezes tomorrow'. The same principle holds good for ocean voyaging, but the effects of successful or inadequate planning are multiplied by the mileage.

Some features of sailing the oceans are obvious. Others less so. For example, nobody brought up in New England would think of crossing the North Atlantic in February aboard anything short of a supertanker. The same would be true for a Norwegian, a Scotsman and, no doubt, a Russian yachtsman from Vladivostok contemplating a trip to Vancouver. Everyone knows that it's cold, it blows like the devil and that without overstating, such a passage could be just plain dangerous. The question of when the voyage might become relatively safe is a matter of passage planning.

Contrary to this obvious scenario, an inexperienced sailor from higher latitudes could be forgiven for imagining the tropics to be a pleasant place where soft zephyrs will caress him gently along from one paradise island to the next. Those who have had the experience will, of course, chuckle up their oilskin sleeves at this naivety. Getting it wrong with the reversing monsoons of the Indian Ocean would be equivalent to an attempt to run up the 'down' escalator at Waterloo

Underground station on crutches.

Planning doesn't end with considerations of the probable wind. There are also currents which affect passage times and morale, fog – creepy even 100 miles from the coast on the Grand Banks of Newfoundland – and ice. More recently, considerations of piracy, demands for cash bonds in exchange for permits to cruise certain areas, and other human factors have also impinged on the sailor's freedom to roam the seas at will. All of the former questions can be answered by available publications. For information on the latter, human factors, more vernacular means must be employed.

The pilot chart and allied publications

The pilot chart

By far the most important aids to ocean voyaging are the month-by-month 'pilot charts' issued by the British Admiralty and the American Defence Mapping authorities. Sometimes known as 'routeing' charts, these comprehensive documents have been produced from countless sightings, observations and readings taken by ships on passage. The information was originally correlated in the nineteenth century by a US Navy lieutenant, whose early results were in high demand amongst clipper ship captains.

A pilot chart is a Mercator projection featuring all the general information a mariner could require for a particular ocean and a given month. This is presented in a graphic form that makes reading it extremely easy. Areas of reliable tradewinds are recognisable at a

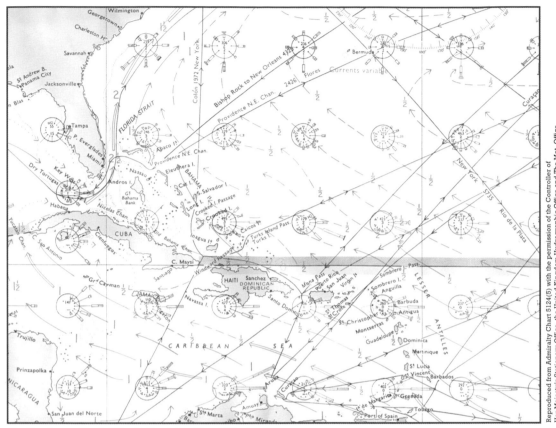

Section from a North Atlantic Routeing Chart (May).

Reproduced from Admiralty Chart 5124(5) with the permission of the Controller of Her Majesty's Stationery Office, the United Kingdom Hydrographic Office and The Met. Office.

glance, for example.

In addition to data on wind direction and strength, these admirable charts also depict magnetic variation (for the year of their issue), currents, typical and specific tracks of tropical revolving storms and mid-latitude depressions, wave heights, fog probabilities, water and air temperatures, as well as mean and extreme ice limits. They even plot the main great circle tracks and note their distances.

If you prefer book format for this information, you might consider the *Atlantic Pilot Atlas* which offers the pilot chart information between two covers. It is, however, more expensive than the US charts.

Wind information

Pilot charts provide the concise wind information vital for small and large sailing craft, with the whole ocean covered by closely spaced 'wind roses'. The British Admiralty wind roses are more comprehensive than the American ones. At their centre, they contain figures indicating the number of observations their data are based upon (a measure of probable reliability). Beneath this is another small figure indicating the percentage of variable winds and a third giving calms. Arranged around each rose's periphery are arrows 'flying with the wind' whose length indicates the percentage of wind from the relevant direction. The nature of the arrow shows the likely wind strengths in the proportions that they have been experienced.

On American pilot charts, the wind arrows give only average wind force and no indication of the number of observations upon which data are based. Nonetheless, they are still of great use and are often more economical to buy.

Use these wind roses for planning a route on the expected month of your passage, but note what is happening on the months either side. Weather is notorious for failure to conform to man's best predictions, so a good guess about what will happen if either you or the developing meteorological pattern is late can avoid disappointment.

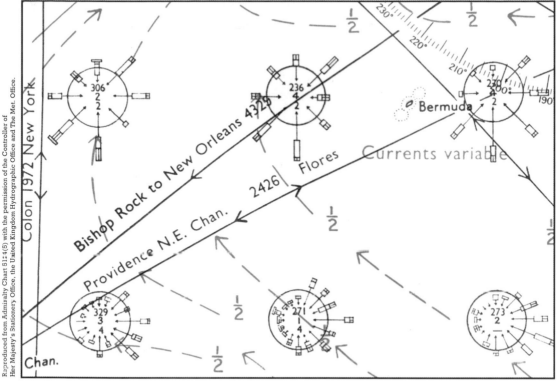

*Wind arrows on a British Admiralty Routeing Chart (May). All details of their coding are given on the chart
itself. Dotted lines indicate current, solid lines steamer routes*

Ocean currents

Paying serious attention to currents can make a
measurable difference in passage times. Half a
knot may not sound much, but it means 12 miles
per day, 85 per week and over 300 in a month.
For a slow-moving vessel, that could be seven or
eight percent of passage time. Double the figure
if you blunder into a counter-current, and you
are looking at a significant difference.

Some currents are very reliable indeed, such
as the North Atlantic Drift once it has swirled
away from the Gulf Stream 'eddies' further west.
Others can be far less so. Once, off the mouth of
the Amazon, I noted a day's run on the log of 140
miles and anticipated the unusual joy of 200
miles between observations. (The pilot chart
placed me firmly in the middle of the hundred-
mile-wide west-bound South Equatorial Current
that swishes along at up to two knots.)
Infuriatingly, my sights revealed a dismal day's
run between observations of a mere 95 miles.
As I sat watching seas that looked like wind-
against-tide in the English Channel, it was
obvious that I was in fact experiencing the
South Equatorial Counter-Current. I made

up my mind to write to their Lordships,
but thought better of it back in port. No doubt
they did their best.

So don't be too disappointed if things fail to
work out as you'd hoped. At least if you have
used these charts and considered the further
information below, you have done all you could.

Ice

The possibility of meeting ice at sea is not
restricted to those who venture into the polar
regions. There are areas in surprisingly low
latitudes into which ice is carried by the current.
The Grand Banks of Newfoundland are a case in
point. Any yacht sailing from the US to northern
Europe must take into account the fact that if she
leaves in May or June, the danger zone inside
the ice limit lies athwart her track. This is clearly
marked on the pilot chart. If your track leads
inside the maximum ice limit you must take the
greatest care to look out and plan a detour if
possible. You would be well advised to keep
clear of the mean limit.

The problem with ice is not so much the
dramatic possibility of crashing into a berg like

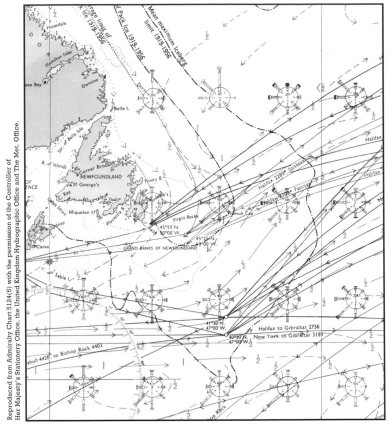

Routeing chart showing pack ice and iceberg limits (May).

While not specific enough to replace the pilot charts, these show wind direction, fog, gale frequency, ice, etc. They can be of considerable value when planning a circum-navigation or for general reference. They should be used in conjunction with Chart no. 5308, also included, which indicates the 'World's Sailing Ship Routes'. Completing the package is chart 5310, 'The World: General Surface Current Distribution'. Employed as a set, these charts can almost plan your trip for you.

The text of the volume itself appears at first to be more relevant to square-riggers than to modern yachts, but it would be an arrogant man who concluded this to be the case. A 'squeaky-clean 38' might slice the wind at 40° in flat water, but once in the big waves off soundings, her crew will be no more keen to point high than that of a four-masted barque who perhaps did not have the option.

When the sailing instructions for a trip to Rio from Europe advise the mariner to pass over a hundred miles to windward of Cabo Sao Roque, they mean what they say. A yachtsman who heeds their advice will have a far more comfortable ride than one who vainly imagines he can sail to windward for a thousand miles and have any friends left on board at the end of it.

On the other hand, in close waters such as leaving the English Channel bound south and ultimately west, it is no longer necessary to work out as far as one can get. So long as Ushant is weathered and a favourable forecast is secured, it is almost always worth 'having a go' at Finisterre in Northern Spain. If the weather fails to develop as you'd hoped, at least there will be somewhere to put in and await an improvement. In the southern hemisphere, particularly in reversing monsoon territory, 'Ocean Passages' is useful in general terms together with its chartlets described above. If nothing else, it will sketch out the big picture and give you a better-than-evens chance of not making any avoidable mistakes.

a latter-day *Titanic*, but rather in running into a 'growler' or a 'bergy bit'. These comparatively small chunks of ice will sink you with ease, yet you could easily miss seeing one if your lookout were casual, even in daylight and good visibility, let alone in fog and darkness. Ice is often associated with fog, so if you have taken a chance, then find yourself plunging onward through dense mist, look out as if your life depended upon it. It could well do just that. Take ice seriously, even if it's not supposed to be part of your trip.

Ocean passages for the world

This Admiralty publication (NP136) used to be the main source of additional information to expand the pilot charts. Second-hand editions will be found in an open-sided cardboard sleeve containing a number of useful chartlets, though in newer editions these are 'bound in'. There are 'World Climatic Charts' (nos. 5301/2) giving large-scale information for the generalised winter and summer months of January and July.

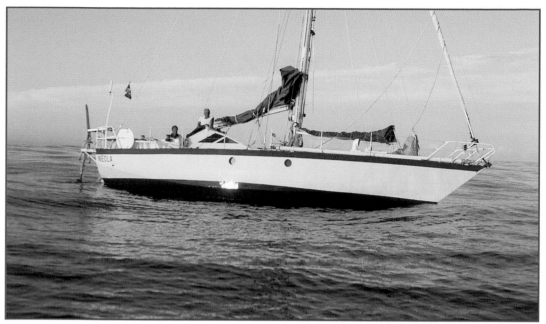

Take as much engine fuel as you possibly can. This yacht is rolling her sails under in the Horse Latitudes, 1000 miles from land and down to her last 10 gallons

World cruising routes

This comprehensive book by Jimmy Cornell is geared specifically to the requirements of the cruising sailor. It recommends optimum times for various routes and offers advice for over 500 in all. In its most recent incarnations it includes data on the Antarctic, and even deals with Spitzbergen for those gallant spirits not seduced by the promise of ever-lasting sunshine in lower latitudes.

The mariner's handbook

You can probably manage without this unless you are planning to visit the ice, but if that should be your intention, buy a copy tomorrow. It is required reading on your subject. If it doesn't put you off, you are the person for the job...

Specific passage guides

The Atlantic Crossing Guide by Anne Hammick is an excellent example of one of these. Such a work is generally comprehensive beyond the bare needs of the navigation plan. Typically, they contain advice on suitable craft, living with the climate, likely provisioning problems and port information, in addition to comprehensive studies of the various crossing options.

Admiralty Pilots contain more information than you might imagine about likely wind and weather patterns. It is always worth shipping one out for your chosen area, and it may help with your landfall if your GPS has died. The descriptions of the world's headlands, cliffs, cities and lighthouses were written for sailors before the electronic age. They have helped me decide where I was on many a precarious morning in time to save my face before the hands began asking awkward questions.

Further sources of data on navigation and other matters

Nowadays, it is hard to find a corner of the globe that nobody has visited. Many people write up their cruises either as articles or in generally available club journals. A good example of these is the Royal Cruising Club annual book of logs, *Roving Commissions*. Accounts of this nature are to be read critically as the writers have generally only a single experience to draw on, but it is still better to listen to somebody who has been to a place than to put to sea with nothing more than a chart on the table.

Anecdotal evidence is often the only assistance available about such matters as piracy. In certain areas this remains a problem to yachts, especially short-handed ones. If unwelcome boarders are a possibility along part of your route, talk to those who may have been on hand, get the buzz, then if violence seems on the cards, treat pirates like hurricanes and go somewhere else.

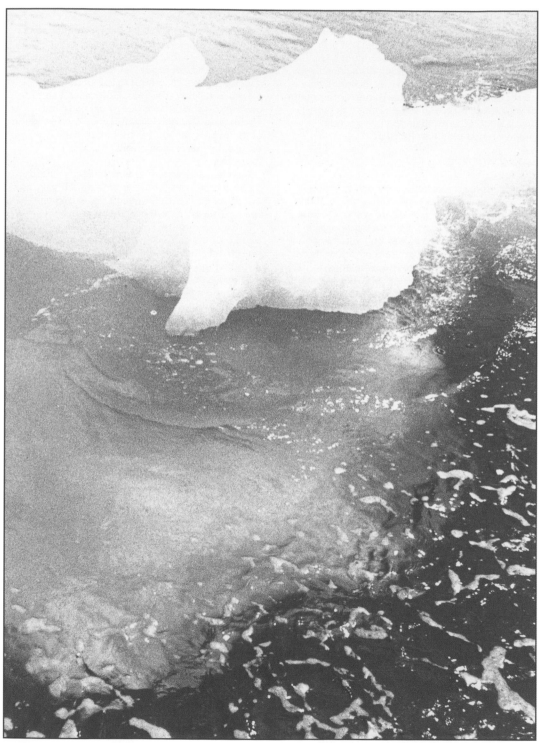

Inside iceberg limits, small growlers can be more dangerous than full sized 'bergs, which are far easier to see. (Photo John Gore-Grimes.)

You will probably pick up wind of any customs problems from keeping your ear to the scuttlebutt. Such books as Cornell's *World Cruising Handbook* will help here, but it is always worth double-checking with consulates or embassies to see if any visas or bonds may be required. To arrive in the Pacific archipelago of your dreams only to be told that you must post a bond of more than you are good for would be bad planning indeed.

Loading Up

A comprehensive commentary on provisioning for ocean voyaging is beyond the scope of this book, but one or two points are worthy of note nonetheless. It can be a daunting proposition to go to the supermarket and buy what you need to feed a crew of even two for a month or more. Four starts to look really expensive and eight does not bear thinking about. My wife generally enters a state of shock as she gropes numbly for the family credit card at the check-out. Yet things are less bad than they may appear. If you multiply the number of people by the days, then think about all the shopping trips you would have made ashore in the same period, you will begin to realise just how much it costs to fuel our bodies.

Regardless of the financial horrors, however, it pays to work out a flexible basic menu to be deployed as appropriate to the weather for every day of the anticipated passage, then multiply the number of days by at least 1.5 to deal with contingencies such as a dismasting. Most meals should be readily prepared with minimum fuss, but one or two more ambitious ones are worth the effort for celebrating birthdays, halfway points, or perhaps even a tight star fix... This should guarantee that you have enough food, luxuries, treats and drinks. And don't skimp on the things you really enjoy and which may be unavailable in the wonderland for which you are bound. Cases of Marmite and curry paste for the Brits, peanut butter for the Americans, and probably foie gras for the French are crucial to long-term morale.One final item about planning a passage which may look obvious is that you should take along all the water you can carry. Don't trust your tanks with your life, either. It makes sense always to ship a substantial amount of water in plastic cans, so that if your tanks fail or become contaminated, all is not lost. Even if you have a water maker, plan for it to break down.

Fuel is slightly different. How much you choose to squeeze into your boat over and above your standard tankfull is really a question of philosophy. If you haven't been out there before, however, you might consider the following.

I have an average fuel tank capacity (80 gallons on a forty-foot boat with a 45HP engine), but on an ocean trip I take all the extra I can reasonable carry without making my boat untidy. Fortunately, I can squeeze around thirty extra gallons under my deck-stowed inverted dinghy which saves me tripping over jerries lashed to the guardrails.

The reason is not that I am impatient and can't stand a few days going nowhere. It's not the waiting that drives you to drink when the wind drops, it's the motion. Sails and booms bang around in the almost ever-present ocean swell as you desperately hang on hoping to get a knot or two out of every catspaw. Your sails chafe, your sheets take a beating and so does your temper. Now is the time your gear will be damaged, not in the gale. It is so much more satisfactory to roll away the headsail, strap in the main and start the engine.

Running at revolutions for four knots or so, most modern diesels are easy companions. They burn surprisingly little fuel compared with the usual muscle-jarring six knots, and all is peace. You find wind more quickly, and there is a further bonus: the four knots of apparent breeze you are creating augments any knot or two that may have been trickling in from the quarter, pulls it round, fills the sails and lets you throttle back even further.

It's a matter of comfort. If that sort of thing is important to you, cram on the cans. If not, you'll just have to put up with it as I did for years, knowing that at least you are next in line with the endless generations of becalmed sailors before you.

19 Making an ocean passage

Taking on an ocean for the first time can be a daunting prospect, yet the statistics tell us that a well-found, properly crewed yacht can voyage for decades without major mishap. So long as the vessel has been selected on the criteria of real seafaring, not some misguided advertiser's flight of fancy, and sensible precautions are taken in the way of spares, tools, victuals and equipment, passage making should be an adventure, not a nightmare.

Given that the boat and her crew are of the right stuff, here is what actually happens:

Beginning a passage

While you are still in harbour, you can generally ensure that your first few days at sea are trouble-free by refusing to leave until satisfied that the weather is going to give you an even break. This isn't always easy. Not only will you yourself be anxious to be gone, you will be met regularly on the dock by stay-at-homes quipping along the lines of, 'What! You still here, then?'

This drives you nuts and makes the task of maintaining crew morale even harder, but you must take it on the chin, because the last thing you want is to begin a 3,000-mile passage with a beat. Sixty miles per day and a drubbing is going to be even worse for the troops than the frustration of being ready and not getting under way.

Once the break comes, I try to leave at a sensible hour of the morning or early afternoon. This gives everyone plenty of daylight to settle down to the motion and the rule of the compass. It's easier that way. I encourage a casual look-out and steering rota until after dinner, then start watches.

Keeping the course

As you sail along your track, be it great circle or equatorial rhumb line, it is highly unlikely that you will benefit from a perfect breeze. It may come from too close ahead, too near dead aft, or too strong on the beam. From time to time you get lucky, but often you'll prefer to modify your ideal heading to take conditions into account. If you end up close-hauled, for example, don't try to stuff the boat up 45° from the true wind. Crack off to 55° or 60°. The breeze won't stay foul for ever and when it changes, the ground you lost will vaporise like morning dew.

The same holds good for the dreaded dead run. Come up a bit and make it into a reach, or at least a comfortable 'boomed-out' course. Similarly, don't be afraid to bear away ten or fifteen degrees to put a steep sea a touch abaft the beam. The wind will change sooner or later and you'll make up the distance again. Comfort is worth a great deal when you've a long way to go.

The downside of wandering with the wind is that if you have carefully worked out a great circle, then find yourself a hundred or two miles north or south of it, you'll just have to sort out a new one. Trying to get back to the original track is a waste of time and distance. Take a fresh departure from wherever you happen to be and keep plugging away until you arrive.

Watch systems

Much has been written about watch systems, so I have only a little to add, possibly because I have a simplistic view. What arrangement you adopt will depend upon whether you have self-steering and how many people are involved.

Two-person partnerships will almost certainly be on auto-pilot. My wife and I have found that either of us can remain alert at night for three hours in normal weather without serious hardship. We read and look out, make a cup of tea and look out, check the course and look out, and so on. Time passes and you have enough of it on your hands for a change to spend some of it thinking. We keep watches during the nominal twelve hours of night, then cruise through the daylight period casually. Watches are shortened in bad weather.

With a crew of three or more who are steering, two hours on the helm works well in decent conditions. 'Two hours on, four off' can allow plenty of rest once you are used to it. If you have four people, 'two hours on, six off' is luxury indeed. In gale conditions, the 'trick' reduces to sixty minutes and on one foggy night in the Greenland Sea while closehauled in force

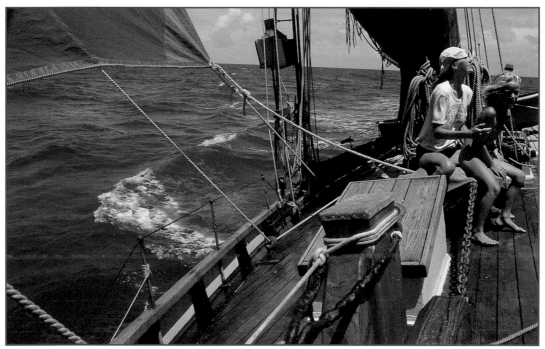

Fair weather, mid-Atlantic, 20°N.

six, the temperature sank so low that we were down to thirty minutes at the helm. The process smacked of torture by sleep deprivation, but we survived and nobody became dangerously cold.

Sometimes with four on board, one of my team will opt to cook for the trip, so the rest of us revert to 'two hours on, four off' for the night hours, with a casual regime during the day, the cook taking a trick from time to time. Another bonus of having a cook is that it is easier to keep meals coming along regularly and reliably. Nothing is so important for a smooth-working ship than the knowledge that however desperate a bully the mate may be, or whatever smells emanate from the skipper's socks, at least breakfast will be a winner as you totter below from your two-hour session in the cold.

Sort out your own watch system, but my advice is to keep it simple. Making up your rest isn't usually a problem at sea, it's just that sleep doesn't come in eight-hour chunks between the silk sheets that some of us would like to be used to.

Ship's Time

In most areas of the globe, the time selected by the local authorities for the people living ashore makes sense for long summer evenings, but does not stack up with real time as set by the sun. You will therefore often set off on passage with your ship's domestic clock keeping a form of daylight-saving time. I prefer my life on the ocean to comply with 'sun time'. It works well with my night watch system.

Once a vessel is on sun time, the question arises as to when this is to be altered as she reels off her longitude. Common sense should prevail here for a private yacht. A sail training vessel may have to be more formal and alter her clocks at the first midnight after entering her next time zone (at $7\frac{1}{2}°$ either side of the Zone Meridians of 0°, 15°, 30°, etc.), though it is more humane to do it at 1800. This is the turn of the old dog-watch when the traditional four-hour watch rota changed sequence with a pair of two-hour 'dogs' between 1600 and 2000. Few yachts today stick with the traditional system, but for many of us six o'clock is still 'happy hour'. A glass of the right stuff will compensate the unfortunate watch that must either bear an extra sixty minutes if sailing one way, or miss the benefit of losing an hour's duty the other.

The navigator's day – ancient mode

The classical yacht navigator's 'day's work' involves a forenoon sight of the sun together with a log reading, followed by a noon sight

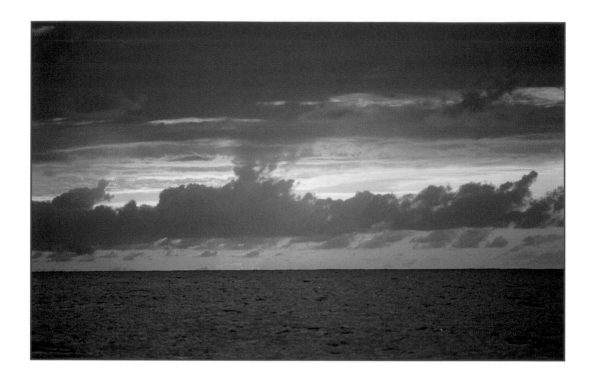

and a transferred position line to provide a fix. This is logged and the distance run from yesterday's position calculated, to the joy or despair of all hands.

If the sky is clear and you are feeling sporty, you might run off a series of stars any evening or morning. This would be executed largely for practice. It is only as landfall approaches that such fixes might become important. Out in the middle, the classical navigator should be perfectly content with the two miles accuracy he might realistically expect on a good day.

And so for centuries forenoon preceded afternoon, the dog-watches led to the first watch, the dead men turned out at midnight for the middle watch, to be replaced by sleepy-eyed shipmates for the grey morning hours. Then the skipper appeared in his slippers early in the forenoon. The noon position preceded lunch yet again. One day followed another until finally the excitement built towards landfall. Would you see the light, or pile up on some ironbound coast? Was that smudge on the horizon really the low-lying shore of a treeless island, or was it a cloud bank coming up to spoil your supper?

Questions such as these plagued us all before GPS arrived to give us a good night's sleep but, my goodness, the satisfaction when what might have been a rising star began to blink 'Group Flash 3 every fifteen seconds'. Life will never be

the same again.

The New Age Ocean Navigator

Now that for most people, astro-navigation is no longer required except for practice, the natural rhythm of the navigator's day has disappeared. We can have a fix any time we want one. I've even caught my crew peeking at how far the ship has to run to Bishop Rock a week out from Cape Cod – before breakfast. Whatever next?

In fact, of course, the navigator's job is vastly simplified. As always, there are two facets to it. The first is working out where you are; the second has always been sorting out how to sail from there to your destination. The former problem is now taken care of, and the latter was always largely common sense. It remains a question of reading the pilot chart in the light of what is actually happening, interpreting the weather reports and considering the sea area into which you have strayed while hunting for a broad reach.

In the new world of instant accurate fixes, I have a feeling that it would be good for discipline (even self-discipline) to ration fixes to one a day, and make it noon. This gives folks something to look forward to, focuses their minds on one of the ancient heartbeats of seafaring, and keeps them in the dark for at least

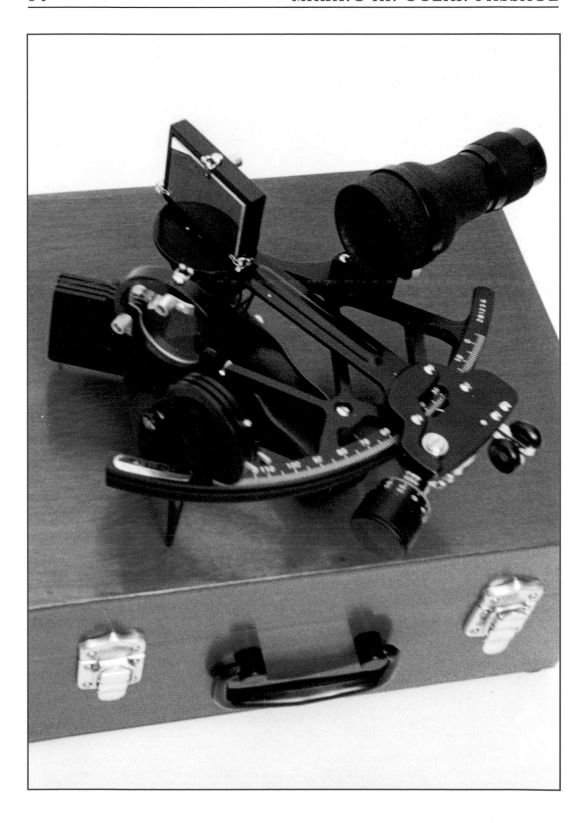

some of the time, a policy favoured by successful pilots from the days of the Yankee clipper to some of the more prudent race navigators of my acquaintance.

One huge advantage of GPS over traditional methods is that at any time you can simply punch the button labelled 'Go To', pick your destination from the waypoints offered by the menu, then read off a distance and a new great circle course. There is no need to programme most receivers to give you a great circle. It is the automatic result of pressing the button. Don't forget that if you choose to ask for it the instrument will also deliver the course in 'magnetic' form, corrected up to the minute — a more satisfactory answer to the ever-varying compass than making a guesstimate from data on a twenty-year-old pilot chart.

Navigators with a through-hull log will probably note its readings at noon. If, like me,

you trail an old-fashioned rotating device, you'll probably prefer to keep the line dry until soundings approach. I once trailed mine all the way to South America and lost two expensive spinners to denizens of the tropic seas — a prodigal waste, experience has taught me...

If your GPS goes down a thousand miles from land and all your back-ups have died from battery leakage or been drowned in a major pooping incident, the least of your troubles will be having to estimate how far you've run since yesterday in order to start up celestial navigation in earnest.

Enjoy your GPS and the freedom from care that it has brought, but do not forget how recently our brotherhood sailed the misty seas in uncertainty, rejoicing in the beauty of our sextants and the constellations they encompassed while remembering every day the motto on the old Air Almanac, *Man is not lost.*

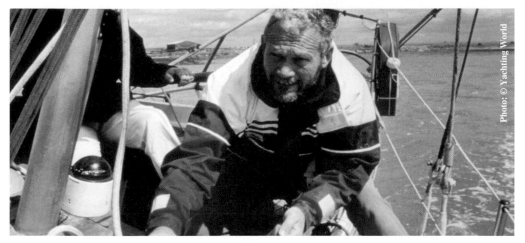

"As sailors, we can always count on volunteer lifeboat crews. Can they count on you? Please join *Offshore* today."

*Sir Robin Knox-Johnston CBE, RD**

However experienced you are at sea, you never know when you'll need the help of a lifeboat crew. But to keep saving lives, the Royal National Lifeboat Institution's volunteer crews need *your* help.

That is why you should join **Offshore**. For just £3.50 per month, you can help save thousands of lives, receive practical information to help keep *you* safe at sea *and* save money on equipment for your boat. *Please join us today.*

Please join *Offshore* – today

Please photocopy and return this form, with your payment if appropriate, to: RNLI, FREEPOST, West Quay Road, Poole, Dorset BH15 1XF.

Mr/Mrs/Miss/Ms [ ] Initial [ ] Surname [ ]

Address [ ]

[ ] Postcode [ ]

I would like to join:

☐ As an *Offshore* member at £ [ ] per month/quarter/year * (min £3.50 per month/£10 per quarter/£40 per year)

☐ As Joint *Offshore* members at £ [ ] per month/quarter/year *

(Husband & Wife, min £6 per month/£17.50 per quarter/£70 per year) * please delete as applicable

Please debit the above sum as indicated from my Visa/MasterCard * now and at the prevailing rate until cancelled by me in writing.

Card No. [ ][ ][ ][ ][ ][ ][ ][ ][ ][ ][ ][ ][ ][ ][ ][ ] Expiry date [/]

Signature [ ] (Please give address of cardholder on a separate piece of paper if different from above.)

Alternatively, I wish to pay my **Offshore** membership by cheque/PO

I enclose a cheque/Postal Order for £ [ ] payable to Royal National Lifeboat Institution.

Or, I wish to pay my subscription by Direct Debit ☐

Please tick the box – a Direct Debit form will be sent to you.   FERN6   Registered Charity No. 209603

Lifeboats
Offshore

Because life's not all plain sailing

© Fernhurst Books 2000

First edition published in 2000 by
Fernhurst Books,
Duke's Path, High Street, Arundel,
West Sussex, BN18 9AJ, England

The first 64 pages of this book were
previously published in modified form and
in black and white as *Celestial Navigation.*

British Library Cataloguing in Publication Data.
A catalogue record for this book is available
from the British Library

ISBN 1 898660 61 1

Printed in Hong Kong
through World Print.

Acknowledgements

The tables on pages 30-39 have been reproduced
from The Nautical Almanac and Sight Reduction
Tables for Air Navigation (AP 3270) Volumes 1
and 3, with permission from data supplied by
HM Nautical Almanac Office, copyright Council
for the Central Laboratory of the Research
Councils. Diagrams on pages 70 and 71 from
Maritime Meteorology with kind permission of
Thomas Reed Publications 0 901281 67 0.
Diagram on page 81 courtesy of Yachting World.

Photographs
The photographs on the pages indicated were
supplied by the following individuals or
agencies. All others by Tom Cunliffe.
Particle Physics & Asronomy Research Council 45,
Ken Pilsbury 68, State University of New York 73,
John Gore-Grimes 89, Vega 94. Cover photo
courtesy of Vega Instruments (distributors of
fine sextants).

Edited by Rosalind Byrne
Artwork by Creative Byte
Cover design by Simon Balley

**For a free, full-colour brochure write,
phone, fax or email us:**

Fernhurst Books, Duke's Path,
High Street, Arundel, West Sussex
BN18 9AJ, United Kingdom
Phone: 01903 882277
Fax: 01903 882715
email: sales@fernhurstbooks.co.uk

RYA and YACHTMASTER are registered trade
marks of the Royal Yachting Association

We are pleased to donate advertising space
within our books to the RNLI. Registered Charity
number 209603.

Ocean Sailing

Tom Cunliffe

fernhurst
B O O K S

www.fernhurstbooks.co.uk